Crime, Punishment
and
Disease

Antony Flew

With a new introduction by the author

Transaction Publishers
New Brunswick (U.S.A.) and London (U.K.)

Third paperback printing 2009

New material this edition copyright © 2002 by Transaction Publishers, New Brunswick, New Jersey. Originally published in 1973 by The Macmillan Press Ltd.

Library of Congress Catalog Number: 2001045688
ISBN: 978-0-7658-0771-7
Printed in the United States of America

Library of Congress Cataloging-in-Publication Data

Flew, Antony, 1923-
   [Crime or disease?]
   Crime, punishment and disease / Antony Flew ; with a new introduction by the author.
      p. cm.
   Originally published: Crime or disease? London : Macmillan, 1973. (New studies in practical philosophy).
    Includes bibliographical references and index.
    ISBN 978-0-7658-0771-7
    1. Psychiatry—Social aspects. 2. Mental illness. 3. Forensic psychiatry. I. Title.

RC454.4 .F583 2001
614.1—dc21
                                                 2001045688

Crime,
Punishment
and
Disease

Contents

To the memory of
RUTH SERUYA DONNISON

Introduction to the Transaction Edition

The present work was originally published in 1973 under the title *Crime or Disease?* and as part of a series of New Studies in Practical Philosophy. Its main object was to make clear the meaning of the expression 'mental disease' and, consequently, to discourage the application of that expression to conditions which do not provide the putative victims of such supposed diseases with a sufficient or even any excuse for failing to act or to refrain from acting in the ways in which they would otherwise have been required to act or to refrain from acting. The need for such clarification was already urgent in 1973. For in the West several senior psychiatrists had for years been maintaining that all crime really is, and/or should be treated as, an expression of mental disease, while in the Soviet Union dissidents abnormal only in their principled and costly dedication to classically liberal ideals were, as compulsory patients in the Serbsky Institute for Forensic Psychiatry, being subjected to what was in practice a form of torture.[1]

Although it is now a decade since the dissolution of the Soviet Union and although most of the psychiatrists quoted in this book are now dead, their ideas still go marching on. Indeed since the first publication of the book these ideas have marched on and out to colonise fresh territories. Where once anti-social behaviour, if it was inhibited at all, was inhibited by some combination of individual self-discipline and external pressures we now have yet another area for medical intervention.

The most important and perhaps the most extensively affected of these new areas of medical intervention is that of primary and secondary education. There today we find psychiatrists regularly prescribing dangerous psychotropic drugs to school children, supposedly to cure various conditions which in earlier times old-fashioned teachers laboured to treat in very different and surely less dangerous ways. And from the fourth edition of the Diagnostic and Statistical Manual of the American Psychiatric Association we can now learn of the Attention/Deficit/Hyperactivity Disorder (ADHD) as well as of the Arithmetic Learning Disorder, the Developmental Expressive Writing Disorder and of the Developmental Reading Disorder; all of which are, apparently, conditions requiring ultimately tax-funded professional psychiatric treatment. All that it is necessary to say here about this increase in the supposed appropriateness of and need for psychiatric treatment of such educational disorders is that it is certainly not to be explained by reference to any accumulation of impressive research evidence revealing the causes of these disorders and/or the effectiveness of their treatment by psychiatrists.[2]

The perennially ignored crux of the whole matter of the relations between crime and disease is that a patient's diseased condition, whether physical or mental, can properly serve as an excuse only in so far as it is to some extent, and relevantly, incapacitating. It is a crux which is chronically confused by the identification of diseases and illnesses with disorders of some other kind. Thus, although Judge Bazclon may himself have appreciated this crucial point, he certainly failed to express it clearly and unequivocally when he formulated what has since been christened the Durham Rule. For that prescribes, "simply that an accused is not criminally responsible if his unlawful act was the *product* of mental disease or defect" (emphasis supplied) while making no mention of any supposedly incapacitating and therefore excusing consequence of being thus diseased or defective.

This crucial point was clearly taken by the American Law Institute. In its Model Penal Code it rules that "A person is not responsible for criminal conduct if at the time of such conduct, as a result of mental disease or defect, *he lacks substantial capacity either to appreciate the criminality of his conduct or to conform his conduct to the requirements of the law*" (emphasis supplied). That is why psychiatrists called to give evidence for the defence labour to persuade the court that the crime was the product of an irresistible impulse.

That is not a conclusion which it is easy, or even perhaps possible, to demonstrate decisively. What is possible, though in the nature of the case not easy, is to demonstrate, by actually inhibiting some extremely strong desire, that that particular desire was not irresistible. But there is no corresponding way of demonstrating that another extremely strong desire which, if resisted at all was certainly not effectively resisted, actually was irresistible. Judges confronted with such psychiatric testimony ought to press these supposedly expert witnesses to reveal their grounds for believing that the defendants' desires to commit their criminal acts were indeed irresistible; and those judges should then go on to ask themselves whether those grounds were sufficient.

Much light can be cast upon this matter by contemplating what is surely the most fundamental distinguishing fact of the human condition. This is the fact that we are all members of a peculiar kind of creatures who each and every one of us can, and therefore cannot but, make choices between the two or more alternative possible courses of action or inaction which are from time to time open to us as individuals. A good place—possibly the best there is—to start to bring out the full significance of this fundamental truth is the great chapter 'Of Power' in John Locke's *Essay Concerning Human Understanding.*[3]

Four characteristically vivid passages can be used to elucidate three closely related concepts: that of being an agent; that of having a choice; and that of being, in the most fundamental sense, able to do otherwise than you actually do do. That most fundamental sense is of course that in which it would have been true for Martin Luther also to say that he could have done otherwise than he did, when he actually said: "Here I stand, I can no other, so help me God." For had Luther actually been struck with a sudden paralysis making him incapable of flight, his stance would have been no credit and no discredit to him. Consider first the two passages immediately below.

1.   This at least I think evident, That we find in our selves a
      power to begin or forbear, continue or end several . . .

motions of our Bodies . . . This *Power* . . . to prefer the
motion of any part of the body to its rest, and vice versa in
any particular instance, is that which we call the *Will*.[4]

2.   Every one, I think, finds in himself a *Power* to begin or
      forebear, continue or put an end to several Actions in
      himself. From the consideration of the extent of this power
      of the mind over the actions of the Man, which everyone
      finds in himself, arise the *Ideas* of *Liberty* and *Necessity*.[5]

In the third passage Locke mistakenly believes himself to
be elucidating the meaning of the expression 'a free agent'
rather than that of 'an agent' simply. In this he was like many
others, both before and since, mistaken. Both those who act
of their own free will and those who act under some kind of
compulsion or constraint are equally agents, choosing to act
as they do act rather than to act in any of the alternative ways
actually open to them. In a fourth passage Locke himself insists that we human beings are all members of a kind of creatures who can and therefore cannot but make choices. These
third and fourth passages are:

3.   We have instances enough, and often more than enough
      in our own Bodies. A man's Heart beats, and the Blood
      circulates, which 'tis not in his Power . . . to stop; and
      therefore in respect of these Motions, where rest depends
      not on his choice . . . he is not a *free agent*. Convulsive
      motions agitate his legs, so that though he *wills* it never so
      much, he cannot . . . stop their motion (as in that odd
      Disease called *Chorea Sancti Viti*,) but he is perpetually
      dancing. He is . . . under as much Necessity of moving, as
      a Stone that falls or a Tennis-ball struck with a Racket.[6]

4.   For it is unavoidably necessary to prefer the doing, or the
      forbearance, of an Action in a Man's power, which is once
      proposed to his thoughts; a Man must necessarily *will* the
      one, or the other of them . . . the act of . . . preferring one
      of the two, being that which he cannot avoid, a Man in
      respect of that act of *willing* is under necessity . . .[7]

With the reminders of these four passages from Locke before us we become equipped to develop ostensive definitions
of two categorically different kinds of bodily movements.

Going deliberately with, rather than against the grain of modern verbal usage, let those bodily movements which can be initiated or suppressed at will be labelled 'movings' and those which cannot 'motions.' Certainly it is obvious that there are plenty of marginal cases. Nevertheless, as long as there are—as there are—far, far more which fall unequivocally upon one side or the other, we must resolutely and stubbornly refuse to be prevented by any such diversionary appeals to the existence of marginal cases from labouring this absolutely fundamental and decisive distinction.

It is in terms of this fundamental distinction between movings and motions that we can now explicate the even more fundamental notion of action, displaying its essential connection with choice. An agent is a creature who, precisely and only in so far as he or she is an agent, can and cannot but make choices: choices between alternative courses of action both or all of which are open; real choices, notwithstanding that sometimes by choosing one or even of any of these open alternatives the agent will incur formidable costs. (If, for instance, as in the film *The Godfather*, instructions were given that you were to be one of those who was to receive an offer which you could not refuse, you could nevertheless refuse; but only at the presumably unacceptable cost of its being your brains rather than your signature on the document signing away your property to the Mafia).

Agents, too, qua agents—it is the price of privilege—inescapably must choose, and can in no way avoid choosing, one of the two or more options which on particular occasions are open and available to them. For once we are confronted with the possibility of action, even a refusal to act can constitute an inaction, a kind of action for which the agent may properly be held responsible. And, furthermore—a point to which we will return—the nerve of the distinction between the movements involved in an action, and those which constitute no more than items or partial components of necessitated behaviour, just is that such behaviour is necessitated, whereas the senses of actions not merely are not, but necessarily cannot be.

Contemplation of the passages just quoted from Locke, and of similar passages should also be sufficient to remind us that we all have the most direct, and the most inexpugnably certain experience: not only both of factual or physical as opposed to logical necessity and of factual or physical as opposed to logical impossibility;[8] but also of both, on some occasions, of being able to do other than we do do and, on other occasions, of being unable to behave in any way other than that in which we are behaving.

We are now equipped to deal with the all too common assumption that the psychological sciences both presuppose and by their findings demonstrate that there is no such thing as freewill. Consequently, it is argued, there is no longer any room for such old-fashioned, conservative ideas as that of moral responsibility. But the ordinary, colloquial usage of the term 'freewill'—the usage which accords with this word's ordinary, non-technical meaning—is in its proper place in such expressions as 'of her own freewill' or 'of their own freewill.'[9] So if anyone either raises the question whether all human beings are as such endowed with freewill or, assuming that we are not, proceeds to draw some alleged consequence, then we must ask them first to explain their technical employment of the term 'freewill' and then to tell us how they think that they know that we are or that we are not endowed with freewill in this new technical understanding of the word 'freewill.'

All those who are quoted in the present work as denying that human beings are endowed with freewill derived this denial from their scientific conviction that every occurrence in the universe must be determined by necessitating causes. Assuming that that is so they went on to conclude that there could be no room in a scientifically instructed world for the idea of moral responsibility. Writing somewhat later, Sir Karl Popper refused, on the very first page of *The Open Universe: An Argument for Indeterminism*, to appeal to "the intuitive idea of freewill: as a rational argument in favour of indeterminism it is useless."[10] Instead he confessed to making a leap of metaphysical belief. For he took his belief in freewill, in his understanding of the word 'freewill,' to be in principle unfalsifiable by any conceivable experience.

But now, the nerve of the categorical distinction between the movings involved in performing an action and the mo-

tions which constitute no more than items or partial components of necessitated behaviour just is that such behaviour is
necessitated whereas actions as such not merely are not but
cannot be. It therefore becomes impossible to maintain the
doctrine of universal physically necessitating determinism, the
doctrine, that is to say, that every movement in the Universe—
including every human bodily movement, the movings as well
as the motions—is determined by physically necessitating
physical causes. The most which can possibly be allowed is
that we are so determined to be people who will in fact choose
to act in whatever senses we do in fact severally choose to act.
The shock of this denial of universal physically necessitating
determinism can perhaps be slightly eased by introducing a
useful and relevant distinction made by David Hume in his
essay 'Of National Characters,' where he wrote:

By *moral* causes, I mean all circumstances, which are fitted
to work on the mind as motives or reasons—By *physical* causes
I mean those qualities of the air and climate, which are supposed to work insensibly on the temper, by altering the tone
and habit of the body . . ." (emphasis original).[11]

A new edition of a book which was first published early in the
nineteen seventies needs to take account of the rise during
the subsequent decades of what can perhaps best be
characterised as an universal subjective relativism. For the
only variety of relativism widespread at that time was a relativism about moral judgements. I myself well remember how
students, especially American students, used to tell me that
all sophisticated people knew that such judgements are *merely*
the social norms of some particular time and place; and then
used almost at once go on, without noticing the apparent inconsistency, to denounce the apartheid regime in South Africa or some other disfavoured person or policy or institution as manifestly and indisputably evil.

Those whom I want to characterise as subjective relativists
and whom I see as protagonists of a New Irrationalism describe themselves in many different ways. They are, they claim,
postmodernists, poststructuralists, or multiculturalists. Sometimes they offer a description peculiar to the field in which
they happen to be operating, such as 'Afrocentrist.' As sub-

jective relativists they hold that every assertion is merely and
nothing but an expression of the asserter's individual or cultural point of view. It therefore has no claim to truth or any
other kind of correctness. This disastrous doctrine is today so
widely accepted that claims that some judgement is, without
relativistic qualification, true or false, right or wrong, good
or bad, rational or irrational, risk being derided as unac-
ceptably naive, parochial and simplistic. Such claims are today not rejected as a preliminary to showing that they are
mistaken, whereas some alternative contention is correct.
They are derided because it is simply assumed that nothing
can be and can be known to be without such subjective qualification true or false, right or wrong. Instead we are all always expressing nothing but our own individual or cultural
points of view.

Of course, and of course revealingly, even the most enthusiastic subjective relativists never even attempt to apply their
general teaching to their own particular, practical, everyday
affairs. When they are seeking answers to questions about the
state of their bank accounts, the scheduled departure and
arrival times of planes, trains or buses, or the effectiveness
and possible side-effects of medical treatments, they take it
absolutely for granted that there can be and usually are answers which can be known to be true.

The fundamental, decisive objection to subjective relativism is that it is self-refuting. For persons maintaining that
subjective relativism is universally true are thereby by implication maintaining that the asserting of this very proposition
by themselves is merely and nothing but an expression of
their own individual or cultural point of view. Since subjectiv-
ist relativism is thus radically incoherent we should not be
surprised to find that it is supported and sustained by invalid
arguments and the collapsing of crucial distinctions.

The favourite form of invalid argument employed here is
that in which from the premise that 'This is that' it is invalidly
inferred that 'This is merely and nothing but that.' Thus C.S.
Lewis in his works of Christian apologetic used to argue—
long before the rise of subjective relativism—that if it were to
be possible to develop a comprehensive physiological account
of how human organisms manage to produce the utterances
and writings which express their beliefs about matters of fact

and real existence, and of their evidencing reasons for holding those beliefs, then it would follow that they could not ever have and know that they had sufficient evidencing reasons to warrant the assertion that any of their beliefs constituted an item of knowledge. The concealed nerve of this argument[12] is that a physiological account of the production of certain uninterpreted sounds and symbols is and must be merely that and nothing but that.

Another simpler example of an argument of the same fallacious form come from the same earlier period and was provided by a leading Freudian psychoanalyst: "To achieve success the analyst must above all be an analyst. That it is to say he must know positively that all human emotional reactions, all human judgements, even reason itself, are but the tools of the unconscious, that such seemingly acute convictions which an intelligent person like this possesses are but the inevitable effect of causes which lie buried in the unconscious level of his psyche."[13] So must that not be true also of this and other judgements of the analysts themselves?

A second favourite form of invalid argument here is that in which in form the premise 'That we can know things only under certain conditions' it is invalidly inferred that 'We cannot know things as they are in themselves.' Various conditions are specified, such 'as they are related to us' and 'under our forms of perception and understanding' and 'in so far as they fall under our conceptual schemes.'

This is a most remarkable argument. For it contrives to mistake conditions needed to make knowledge possible for conditions making it impossible. It is perhaps even more remarkable in as much as it appears to have seduced Immanuel Kant.[14]

There is a third form of invalid argument which despite its surely quite obvious invalidity is nevertheless commonly found among those claiming to be postmodernists, poststructuralists, multiculturalists and the like. This is the argument which from the premise that 'Some or many so and sos are such and such' proceeds immediately to infer that 'All so and sos are such and such.'[15] Thus, in such circles it is argued that, because what is accepted as, or passes for, a known fact is sometimes later discovered not to have been, therefore there is no such thing as knowledge and are no such things as facts. When this 'passes for' argument is clearly stated its fallaciousness is, or ought to be, blindingly obvious.

Usually, however, as shorthand for 'what is accepted as knowledge' and 'what passes for truth' the New Irrationalists write 'knowledge' or 'truth,' putting these key words between sneer quotes. They thus neutralise the implications of epistemic success ordinarily carried by these words. For knowledge must be of what is true, but 'knowledge' (knowledge between sneer quotes) need not be. Facts must be facts, but 'facts' (facts between sneer quotes) need not be. As the sneer quotes become ubiquitous the crucial difference between truth and knowledge and so-called truth (truth between sneer notes) and so-called knowledge (knowledge between sneer quotes) is forgotten. So the passes for fallacy starts to sound like a valid argument instead of the self-refuting non sequitur which it really is.

Something has finally to be said here about the 'deprogramming' of people allegedly 'brainwashed' into conversion to various usually new minted 'cult religions' such as Hare Krishna or the Unification Church founded by the Reverend Sun Myung Moon (the Moonies). For complaints about conversions began to be heard from relations of the converts and calls for their 'deprogramming' shortly after the first publication of *Crime or Disease?* For us the first question has to be 'What is meant by 'brainwashing' and would someone's conversion by this means justify the application to them, if necessary under constraint, of some other treatment designed to secure the reversal of the conversion originally effected by this method?"

That this is indeed the question comes out very clearly from a letter, written by a spokesperson for FAIR, "the organisation set up to help the families of young people caught up in cult religions," and in *The Nursing Mirror* (July 30, 1979). Under the headline "Beware the 'brainwashing' religious cults," this correspondent argued that "without programming there would be no need of deprogramming!" The letter continued:

> The methods used by these pseudo-religious cults are a dangerous misuse of psychology . . . There are many reports by . . . experts in

mental health of the effects on the mind caused by a cult's programming and the obvious conclusion to be drawn . . . is that
deprogramming, carried out properly and sympathetically, is the
only possible way of restoring the individuality of a convert and his
ability to think and act freely.

There is no need here to dispute the hypothetical contention that—were it once granted that certain people had been
converted to new systems of belief when physically confined,
and by the use of drugs, violence, starvation, sleep-depriva-
tion or other manifestly improper means—then it might well
become licit to employ similar, normally unacceptable means
in the attempt to restore their previous condition. Fortunately
that difficult question does not in the present case arise. Certainly the enemies of the various minuscule sets that those
enemies like to call "cult religions," or "pseudoreligious cults,"
are very free with vivid, metaphorical charges or soul-snatch-
ing, mental rape, mind-thievery, brainwashing and the like.
They appear nevertheless unable or unwilling to spell out
any literal, specific and suitably scandalous content for all
this scarifying abuse.

For example, Ferdinand Mount, a journalist more genuinely critical than most, put a key question in *The Spectator*
(July 4, 1981): "But is there really a distinction in kind between the Moonies' methods of indoctrination and conversion and the methods of recognised religions?" He got no
answer either from FAIR or from anyone else, either in private or published in the letters columns of that magazine.
But I myself was able to add a further contribution there:
"Like most of those who have participated in academic conferences organised and financed by the cultural foundation
established by the Unification Church I have received many
letters of private protest. To every one I have replied with an
assertion and a question: the assertion, that the conferences I
have attended were all conducted with absolute academic
propriety; and the question, what outrageous and peculiar
methods persuasion employed by the Moonies are being de-
nounced as 'brainwashing'? No correspondent has ever given
me a clear and definite answer revealing any firm basis for
that accusation.

There is here, endemic, a crucial equivocation. Where
charges are being brought against disfavoured religious

organisations, the word 'brainwashing' is intended to carry implications of well nigh if not altogether irresistible pressures, with suggestions of the cruel and unusual techniques employed by the Chinese Communists on helpless prisoners captured in the Korean War. But when evidence is demanded to justify such charges, we find that the word is once more being construed only in its weaker sense—the sense in which it has become commonplace to speak of anyone accepting some position considered by the speaker to be altogether irrational and preposterous as having been brainwashed into that acceptance.

Yet we cannot simply leave things there, with a strong warning about the ambiguity of the term 'brainwashing.' For in the United States at least one person had made a successful professional career out of selling his services as a deprogrammer to the relatives of supposedly brainwashed converts before any checks began to be put upon such amateur psychiatric treatment of very far from voluntary patients.

Consider, for instance, his publisher's advertisement for Ted Patrick's *Let Our Children Go:* "Patrick is the man whose profession is the rescuing of brainwashed youngsters from cults like Hare Krishna and Sun Myung Moon. With their parents' help he snatches them off the street and takes them to a hideout to deprogram them. He almost always succeeds—has saved more than 1,000—and the youngsters themselves are intensely grateful. Now he tells us how does it."[16]

Mr. Patrick himself, who is not by any standards psychiatrically qualified, and who had been operating without the protection of the law, was in September 1980 sentenced by the San Diego Superior Court to one year's imprisonment, five years probation, and a fine of $5,000. According to the *International Herald Tribune* of September 20, 1980, this sentence was for Patrick's part "in the kidnapping of a twenty- five year old Tucson waitress whose family feared that she was controlled by a religious zealot. Judge Norbert Ehrenreund ruled, "We must observe the law that makes it a crime to abduct another human being." Allowing that Patrick had done a deal of good work, the judge insisted nevertheless: "There must be no further deprogramming. That part of his life must exist no longer."

This, however, was by no means the end of the affair. For others had been and still are labouring to secure the protection of the law for the confinement of converts to such disfavoured religious systems and for their compulsory subjection to the deprogramming treatment. Some qualified psychiatrists are also arguing that conversions to disfavoured minority belief systems fall within their own professional bailiwick, and should therefore be diagnosed and treated by and only by themselves and their colleagues. The effort to obtain legal sanction for forcible deprogramming takes the form of either appeals to existing laws, or moves to introduce new laws, under which converts can or could be made wards of some other members of their families, who then will, or would, with the full backing of the state power, see to it that the convert gets the treatment. This treatment is in fact, to put it mildly, harsh, while everyone, most especially including the patient, must know that, once they have been so confined, there will be no escape either from the legal guardianship or from that harsh treatment until and unless the deprogrammers become persuaded that they have effected a sound and thorough deconversion.

The psychiatric argument is that the original conversion has to be diagnosed as either being, or being symptomatic of, a freshly identified syndrome for which the uncomfortably Anglo-Saxon label 'faith sickness' has been suggested. Since it is an illness it must be bad for the patient. After all, as Ted Patrick, said, when it is all over, "the youngsters themselves" say that they "are intensely grateful."

Since it is, surely, the criterion of the soundness of a deprogramming job that those deprogrammed should be content in the belief system to which they have reverted, any Englishman of my generation must here by reminded of the immortal words of Miss Amanda (Mandy) Rice-Davies, summoned to give evidence in a judicial inquiry into a political scandal with supposed implications for national security. When told of men who had denied her assertions about their joint sexual activities, she responded with decisive finality: "Well, they would, wouldn't they?"

ANTONY FLEW

Notes

1. See Sidney Block and Peter Reddaway *Russia's Political Hospitals* (London: Victor Gollancz, 1977). It is unfortunate that nowhere in this otherwise highly commendable work is there any clear statement of the crucially relevant difference between statistical normality, which is indeed socially relative, and prescriptive normality, which surely is not. For relevant discussion see 'Mental health, mental disease, mental illness: "the medical model"' in Philip Bean (Ed.) *Mental Illness: Changes and Trends* (New York: John Wiley, 1983).

2. Though many would prefer a work more systematic and less polemical, anyone concerned about the relentless rise of psychiatry and the consequences of that rise must come to terms with Bruce Wiseman, *Psychiatry: The Ultimate Betrayal* (Los Angeles: Freedom Publishing, 1995). See also Stanton Peele, *Diseasing of America: Addiction Treatment out of Control* (Lexington, MA: D.C. Health, 1989).

3. The now standard addition is that edited by P. H. Nidditch (Oxford: Clarendon, 1975).

4. II (xxi) 5, p.236

5. Ibid., 7, p.237.

6. Ibid., 11, p.239. The Latin means 'St. Vitus's Dance.'

7. Ibid., 23, pp. 245-6.

8. This is where the philosopher David Hume could have found the impressions from which the ideas of factual necessity and factual impossibility can be derived. See for instance, my 'Legitimation of Factual Necessity,' in J.J. MacIntosh and H.A. Meynell, *Faith, Scepticism and Personal Identity* (Calgary: University of Calgary Press, 1994), pp. 101-117 or, more recently, my 'Second thoughts about the *First Enquiry* in *Philosophical Writings*,' No. 10, Spring 1999, pp.89-91.

9. In the fourteenth section of the chapter from which the four quotations above are drawn Locke himself insisted that the question "*Whether Man's Will be free, or no* . . . is altogether improper; and it is as insignificant to ask, whether a Man's *Will* be free, as to ask, whether his Sleep be Swift, or his Vertue square . . ."

10. (London: Hutchinon, 1982). For arguments about the ways in which Popper was misled to this conclusion, see my 'Popper's Cartesian Inheritance,' in *Philosophical Writings*, No. 4, January 1999, pp. 81-89.

11. *Essays Moral, Political, and Literary* edited by E.F. Miller (Indianapolis, IN: Liberty Classics, 1985). p.198.

12. For a fuller account of that argument, and for some discussion of some associated arguments, see my *A Rational Animal and other Philosophical Essays on the Nature of Man* (Oxford: Clarendon, 1978), Ch. 5.

13. Charles Berg, *Deep Analysis* (London: Allen and Unwin, 1946), p.190.

14. See on this David Stove's mischievous masterpiece *The Plato Cult and Other Philosophical Follies* (Oxford: Blackwell, 1991), Ch. 5 and 6.

15. For a first class treatment of the New Irrationalism in all its forms, see Susan Haack, *Manifesto of a Passionate Moderate* (Chicago and London: University of Chicago Press, 1998).

16. Ted Patrick, *Let Our Children Go* (New York: Ballantine, 1977).

Updating Notes

When a book first published many years ago in the United Kingdom (UK) is reissued in the USA, the Second Edition needs at least some explanatory notes. Since it was impractical to insert these additions among the original endnotes, they are collected here:

p. 27 grumbling appendix: This expression is in England popularly supplied to an uncomfortable condition of the vermiform appendix.

p. 31 summun bonum: This is Latin for 'the supreme good.'

p. 40 pre-conquest days: This is a reference to the period before the end of World War II, after which Hungary and Rumania were both among the states occupied by the armed forces of the USSR until puppet governments had been firmly established.

p. 41 table-tennis contests: The first sporting achievement of the Communist regime established in China in 1949 was to produce a large number of formidably skilful female table-tennis players.

p. 41 traditional Kikuyu society: The Kikuyu are the dominant tribe in Kenya, and female circumcision is a traditional institution of that tribe.

p. 56 Broadmoor: This is the main UK institution for the confinement and, hopefully, treatment of the criminally insane.

p. 66 Classical knowledge: The reference here is to the Greco-Roman classics, from one of which, for instance, the name of the Oedipus of the Oedipus Complex was derived.

p. 83 *Dennison v State* (1966): My hope that the case of Stephen Dennison was and would remain unparalleled has been disappointed. For on 8 September 1983 the *Daily Telegraph* of London reported that a Mental Health Tribunal had ruled that "A 51-year old man who has spent 35 years in mental hospitals, 30 of them in Moss Side, Liverpool's top security hospital, can return to the outside world." His name was Peter Wilson and he was first incarcerated in a mental health institution after, at the age of 15. "He had run away from home and was said to be out of the control of his parents . . . He was sent to Moss Side five years later after breaking windows to get into a beach hut."

p. 97 *Crime as Destiny:* The German original was *Verbrech en als Schicksal, Studien an Kriminellen Zwillingen* (Leipzig: Georg Thieme Verlag, 1929). *Crime as Destiny* (London: George Allen and Unwin, 1931) had a foreword by Haldane and was translated by his wife. It was reprinted in 1996 by Scott-Townsend Publishers in Washington DC. Despite Haldane's enthusiastic endorsement, Lange's findings seem to have been overshadowed by most later investigators.

My remarks about J.B.S. Haldane's involvement with the Communist Party were perhaps too generous. For the relevant volume of the *Dictionary of National Biography* tells us that he joined the Communist Party in 1942, that he resigned on some date unrevealed but "c.1950," and that this resignation was "because of Stalin's interference with science." In view of the facts that Haldane was Britain's leading geneticist, and that the Lysenko affair reached its climax in 1940-1 with the dispatch to the Gulag of Academician N.I. Vavilov, the Soviet Union's and surely then the world's leading geneticist, the dates of both Haldane's joining the Communist Party and of his leaving it are remarkably late.

For information about the nature and extent of Stalin's 'interference' with science and with so much else in the years up to 1940-1 see Robert Conquest *The Great Terror* (London and Melbourne: Macmillan, 1968). For preference see it in the second edition, which contains a substantial new introduction written by the author after the collapse of the Soviet regime.

p. 118 Note 6. The proprietor of *The Times* of London during the period in question was a Canadian named Thompson.

p. 118 Note 7. The Latin translates into: "for, when gathered, I flung them away, my only feast in it being my own sin, which I was pleased to enjoy."

p. 123 Note 55. 'The Vicar of Bray' was the name both of a popular (probably early eighteenth century) song and of the anti-hero of that song. Its story is derived from that of a time-serving sixteenth century Vicar of Bray in Berkshire, England who managed to retain his living during all the changes in the state religion through the reigns of Henry VIII, Edward VI, Mary and Elizabeth I.

> And this is the law I will maintain,
> Until my dying day, Sir,
> That whatsoever king shall reign,
> I'll still be the Vicar of Bray, Sir.

Editor's Foreword

In this monograph, Professor Flew discusses a question which is of the greatest interest and the first importance from both a philosophical and a practical point of view. The correct analysis of the concept of responsibility and punishment has long been sought by philosophers and in this monograph one aspect of that quest is brought right up to date. A proper treatment, unimpaired by confusions of mind or errors of fact, society's delinquents is held by all morally responsible people to be desirable and this monograph seeks to guide us towards that end.

Professor Flew discusses his subject with a characteristic wealth of documentation and clearness of thought. His conclusions are not reached dogmatically and his hope that this book will stimulate further discussion is bound to be fulfilled. Into an area so frequently darkened by prejudice, whether of the reactionary or the radical variety, it sheds much light.

University of Exeter   W. D. HUDSON

The mentally ill, far from being guilty persons who merit punishment, are sick people whose miserable state deserves all the consideration due to suffering humanity.

PHILIPPE PINEL (1745–1826)

There is a way of thinking and feeling about punishment, not uncommon in our days, which exhibits a high degree of inconsistency. It more or less explicitly accepts the doctrine that crime (all or some of it) is mere disease. . . . And, rightly from this ground, a protest is made against such unwilled defects being imputed and judged of morally. . . . Justice is the assignment of benefit and injury according to desert; but this man is not a moral agent . . . surely what follows is that justice is indifferent to his case. What is just or unjust has surely nothing to do with our disposal of his destiny.

F. H. BRADLEY (1846–1924)

Must the psychiatrist then unseat the king and actualize in the realm of fact the 'philosopher-king' of Plato's imagination? . . . if sufficiently secure in his knowledge of himself and of his field, he may dare where others dared and lost before.

HAROLD LASSWELL (1902–   )

Preface

It is nowadays very common to assume, to suggest, or even to say, that some, or most, or even all, crime against the public laws, or more private moral defect, or other untowardness in human behaviour, is a symptom of mental disease. The aims of the present essay are: first to investigate the meanings and implications of such claims; second to emphasise what consequently has to be made out if their acceptance is to be warranted; and third to correct a few of the more popular mistakes encouraging the misconception that psychological inquiries have already established a much more comprehensive and less qualified conclusion here than they in fact have – or ever could.

Some of what I have to say might, with appropriate alterations, be applied also to parallel theses representing some or all delinquencies as symptoms not of mental disease but of social. Theses of this second sort are collectivist, whereas those with which we shall be concerned put the emphasis in the first place upon the individual. It is therefore both interesting and significant that in Dostoievsky's *Crime and Punishment* there appears to be only one reference to ideas of our first kind. This occurs in Section 6 of Part I, where Raskolnikov reflects on his conviction that an 'eclipse of reason and loss of will-power attacked a man like some disease, developed gradually, and reached its climax a short time before the crime was actually committed; it continued the same way at the moment of the crime and for a short time afterwards, according to each individual; then it passed off like any other disease'.

What is much more typical of the advanced notions found in that book is the conversation reported in Section 5 of Part III by Raskolnikov's student or ex-student friend Razumikhin: 'It all began with the point of view of the socialists. Their point of view is well known: crime is a protest against bad and abnormal social conditions and nothing more. No other causes are admitted. Nothing! . . . Environment is the root of all evil – and nothing else! A favourite phrase. And the direct consequence of it is that if society is organised on normal lines, all crimes will vanish at once, for there will be nothing to protest against, and all men will become righteous in the twinkling of an eye.'

Such social theses may of course be combined with those of the more individualistic kind to be considered here. Thus in the Preface to *The Psychoanalytical Approach to Juvenile Delinquency*, that formidable Freudian Dr Kate Friedlander, after excoriating what are supposed to be the mere rationalisations of law-abiding but psychologically unenlightened citizens, tosses off the remarks: that 'they probably do not know that delinquency is a disease of society, just as cancer, for instance, is a disease of the individual'; and that 'in the long run the delinquent himself suffers by his anti-social behaviour much more than society'.

Part I is intended both to provide historical perspective and to display the main logical links between the various key notions. If we are to know where we are in complex terrain we need above all a sketch-map, showing just the main features and how these relate to one another.

Part II develops the contention that the notion of mental disease should be approached by way of that of physical disease – what would once have been called disease, without prefix or suffix. This simple-minded emphasis happens to be much less commonplace than we might expect. Although everyone takes it for granted when exculpation is in question that the assertion that this is a case of mental disease must license most of the inferences which would be authorised by a corresponding claim about physical disease, this crucial and straightforward assumption seems to be almost universally overlooked when the time comes to ask what is, or ought to be, meant by 'mental disease' and 'mental health'.

Part III confronts directly those general deterministic assumptions which mislead so many into believing – or into believing that they ought to believe – some all-embracing conclusion about all delinquencies being expressions of psychological disorder; and hence, because everyone in this context employs the word 'disorder' to mean something of which the subject is a victim, as more or less venial – if not actually and strictly uncontrollable. My own rather pedestrian guiding idea here is that some truths are so unshakeably certain that in any conflict the give must always be on the other side. It is the approach suggested, in another sphere, by Abraham Lincoln: 'If slavery is not wrong, nothing is wrong.'[1]

When I contributed *Evolutionary Ethics* to an earlier series organised by Dr Hudson my hope was to produce the definitive monograph. I shall by contrast measure any success of the present essay mainly by whatever contribution it makes to its own replacement. In particular, although I am sure that my approach from the physical paradigms of disease and health is right, I am equally sure that my realisation of it must be relevantly defective. A general awareness of fallibility is in this case reinforced by recognising a particular handicap. For very little work seems to have been done on the philosophical analysis of these paradigms. Some may recall a sharp remark made in Section 28 of the Seventh Dialogue of Berkeley's *Alciphron*: 'Vice, indolence, faction, and fashion produce minute philosophers, and mere petulancy not a few.' Certainly no one who has ever attended a conference of professional philosophers can be in any doubt of the truth of at least the last clause of this psychological analysis. Yet we should also notice that philosophy is pre-eminently a subject which advances most easily through the correction and improvement of earlier attempts.

What is to be done is, as the series title promises, philosophical. Nevertheless, as the series title again promises, this philosophy is not cloistered. Certainly I hope that the present study, and indeed the whole series, will be found to be of some value by people whose interests are primarily practical: it was, I believe, a genuine scandal to philosophy that in the great sweep of her survey of *Social Science and Social Pathology* Lady Wootton should have been able to find only one debt to acknowledge to a philosopher.[2] This desire to be if possible useful has encouraged a fuller and more leisurely exposition than would have been appropriate in a work for philosophers only: thus Part 1 would have been shorter, and surely duller, had it been addressed primarily to colleagues. In order to underline both this relevance and my own practical concern I have quoted from and referred to criminological literature very lavishly; and I have accepted the consequence that the notes must be correspondingly lavish.

I have dedicated this book to the memory of my mother-in-law Ruth Seruya Donnison. It was her enthusiasm for her work as a justice of the peace in Berkshire, as well as her earlier efforts to introduce better methods of dealing with young offenders in Burma, which inspired my own now nearly twenty-year-old first venture into this field of theory.[3]

I owe my warm thanks to the departmental secretaries who put my material into readable typescript: Mrs Rita Lee at Keele, and Mrs Rhoda Blythe at Calgary. I should also like to express my obligation to members of the Library staffs at Keele and Calgary, who helped me in tracking down sources and verifying references.

ANTONY FLEW

The University of Calgary,
Alberta, Canada

I A Survey of the Logical Geography

I   In an investigation of meaning it is best to begin from the strongest thesis. For, although some hedged and qualified version is more likely to be defensible as true, the understanding of the meaning of any such weaker thesis presupposes the understanding of the meaning of its stronger relative. For example, although the guarded and cautious 'It looks to me like a B-52' commits the speaker to less than the categorical and unqualified 'It is a B-52', the former is both semantically more sophisticated than the latter and logically parasitical upon it. You could not, that is to say, understand what is meant by 'It looks to me like a B-52' if you did not already know the meaning of 'It is a B-52'.

A second illustration may help to bring this very fundamental point out more clearly. This illustration is drawn from Part v of Descartes' *Discourse on the Method*: which, in view of the relevance to the criticism of the Cartesian programme of systematic doubt of the consideration which it illustrates, is apt. Descartes there has just described the physiological discoveries of Harvey. He proceeds to suggest: not that the brutes, and the bodies of human beings, look like, and so might be mistaken for, machines – for surely they do not, and scarcely could; but rather that his recommendation is that we should 'think of these as' machines, 'which, having been made by the hands of God, are incomparably better arranged and possess in themselves movements more admirable than any of those which can be invented by men'. Now perhaps Descartes himself did not appreciate the exact significance of what he wrote here. But certainly – returning visibly to our muttons – there is a world of difference: between on the one hand maintaining unreservedly that all crime is a symptom of some mental disease; and on the other hand maintaining only that it should be thought of, or regarded, as such. The second of these two possible claims is, in the senses

indicated in the previous paragraph, both semantically more
sophisticated than the first, and logically parasitical upon it.
For if I announce that I will, perhaps for certain purposes only,
deem you to be, or regard you as being, married, or a com-
patriot, or a human being, or a mental patient, or what have
you, then I am precisely not saying that you truly are. Rather
I am taking it absolutely for granted that you are truly not.
What otherwise would be the point of my being so graciously
willing to deem the contrary?

It will not do therefore to take as our text anything which
even hints at limitation. Instead we need a perfectly explicit
and completely comprehensive statement. For this purpose it
would be hard to better what was said by Dr J. R. Rees, who
served at various times as Medical Director of the Tavistock
Clinic in London, President of the World Federation for Mental
Health, and Honorary Consulting Psychiatrist to the British
Army. In his Clarke Hall Lecture on *Mental Health and the
Offender* he insisted: 'It should be stressed that all failure to
comply with the rules of the game, and indeed all anti-social
behaviour, whether it is noticed merely in the nursery or comes
eventually to the courts of the country, is evidence of some
psychological failure in the conduct of life. Crime (behaviour
which is prohibited by the criminal code) is the outward manifestation or sign of some disorder in the personality and character, however that may have been caused.'[4]

This bold statement can be paired with an even bolder confession from the other side of the Atlantic. Dr Karl Menninger,
one of America's most distinguished psychiatrists, in his book
The Crime of Punishment maintains:

> The very word 'justice' irritates scientists. No surgeon ex-
> pects to be asked if an operation for cancer is just or not. No
> doctor will be reproached on the grounds that the dose of
> penicillin he has prescribed is less or more than justice would
> stipulate. Behavioral scientists regard it as equally absurd to
> invoke the question of justice in deciding what to do with a
> woman who cannot resist her propensity to shoplift, or with
> a man who cannot resist an impulse to assault somebody.
> This sort of behavior has to be controlled; it has to be dis-
> couraged; it has to be stopped. This (to the scientist) is a
> matter of public safety and amicable coexistence, not of
> justice.[5]

It is only fair to Dr Rees to add now that, having said what he has just said categorically and without any qualification, he forthwith proceeds to deny some of the clear implications of his own assertion: 'Please do not think that in my mind there is any feeling that all offenders, such as those who drive too fast in controlled areas, or those who switch on their fires during a fuel cut, need to be referred to a psychiatrist or studied by him.' Notice here also that Dr Menninger too cheats by illustrating his most provocative contentions only with examples so specified as to be uncontroversial: 'a woman who cannot resist her propensity to shoplift'; and 'a man who cannot resist an impulse to assault somebody'.

We shall in Part III be considering the significance of this fact, that even such prophets of psychiatry as Dr Rees and Dr Menninger seem thus themselves to be unable to live with the logical consequences of what they take to be the presuppositions and the implications of their discipline. But our immediate concern is with the Rees thesis itself: 'that all failure to comply with the rules of the game, and indeed all anti-social behaviour, . . . is evidence of some psychological failure in the conduct of life. Crime . . . is the outward manifestation or sign of some disorder in the personality and character, however that may have been caused.'

*

2   In interpreting any such contention it is necessary to distinguish, from the beginning: between on the one hand claims which are supposed to be true as a matter of contingent fact; and on the other hand claims which are verified as logically necessary simply and solely by reference to the meanings of the terms involved. A good stock illustration of this distinction can be derived from Shakespeare. After he has seen his father's ghost Hamlet pretends to reveal a secret to Horatio and Marcellus (Act I, Sc. 5):

> There's ne'er a villain living in all Denmark
> But he's an arrant knave.

Horatio replies:

> There needs no ghost, my lord, come from the grave
> To tell us this.

The reason why Hamlet's 'relevation' is no relevation at all is that what he is saying is logically necessary. It could be known to be true by anyone knowing the meaning of the sentence in which it is expressed, and anyone venturing to contradict him would thereby involve himself in self-contradiction.

Suppose instead that Shakespeare – defying simultaneously the demands of both drama and metre – had made Hamlet maintain that all Danish villains were the products of broken homes. This anachronistic contention would have been a logically contingent proposition. If anyone were to contradict it he would not thereby and necessarily involve himself in self-contradiction. To know whether it was true or false it would not be sufficient to appreciate only what it meant. Some reference would have to be made to sociological studies of the home backgrounds of Danish villains.

In this stock, imaginary illustration the logically necessary proposition is analytic, tautological and trifling. But other, actual examples are both relevant and far from trifling. For instance: while suicide was still under English law a crime it seems to have become a convention for coroners' courts – despite sometimes the clearest evidence to the contrary – to insist that, if someone suicided, then he must have been at the moment when he did the deed of unsound or disordered mind. By such insistence suicide became in effect a criterion for mental disorder. The mere fact that he did suicide was construed as a sufficient condition of his having been, at least temporarily, of unsound mind. In this interpretation to say that at the time of his suicide the balance of his mind was disturbed must be a tautology. But the object of the exercise was to justify a verdict in which the same form of words would be quite differently interpreted. For while the law remained what it then was a verdict without this saving rider involved both legal and other consequences which to their credit all concerned wished to avoid – even at the cost of a measure of what privately within the legal profession was dubbed 'pious perjury'.

The same logical points are illustrated in a complementary but more mischievous example, drawn from Joseph Heller's novel *Catch-22* (chapter 5):

'Sure there's a catch,' Doc Daneeka replied, 'Catch-22. Anyone who wants to get out of combat duty isn't really crazy.' There was only one catch and that was Catch-22, which specified that a concern for one's own safety in the face of dangers that were real and immediate was the process of a rational mind. Orr was crazy and could be grounded. All he had to do was to ask; and as soon as he did, he would no longer be crazy and would have to fly more missions. . . . Yossarian was moved very deeply by the absolute simplicity of this clause. . . . 'That's some catch, that Catch-22,' he observed. 'It's the best there is,' Doc Daneeka agreed.

*

3   Given the distinction made in the previous section it becomes clear that the Rees thesis could be taken in two different ways. What is surely the intended interpretation is that all the various forms of delinquency mentioned are, as a matter of contingent fact, manifestations of mental disorder; where the criteria determining what is or is not a crime, or whatever, are entirely independent of the criteria determining whether a person is or is not mentally disordered. Alternatively the thesis might – although this is here a most implausible construction – be read as a covert confession that for Rees the occurrence of any sort of delinquent behaviour is a criterion for psychological derangement; and hence that, for Rees, any claim that any offender, against whatever standard, was of unsound mind would be sufficiently and very easily justified as tautological.

Begin with the former interpretation. This procedure is the more fitting since such boldly comprehensive contentions are typically first urged as unequivocally contingent. It is only when their forward positions have been overwhelmed by objections that the too resolute defenders withdraw to citadels made tautologically impregnable. Speaking literally, this is what would have happened if someone who had started by asserting, in a straightforward sense, that only madmen kill themselves; had then been forced by opposition to recognise many cases in which men, who were surely in that ordinary interpretation sane, have suicided as the result of coolly rational deliberation; and had then reacted, not by frankly admitting his error, but by maintaining instead that anyone who kills himself must be, by that very token, mad. The danger of such a reaction is of course that the stubborn defender, and perhaps others also, will assume that he has by this manœuvre successfully maintained his original position; and that then, equivocating between two radically different interpretations of the same form of words, they will all take it that a tailor-made tautology licenses the inference which would indeed be warranted had he really established his first contention.

Rees asserts: 'Crime (behaviour which is prohibited by the criminal code) is the outward manifestation of some disorder in the personality and character. . . .' By providing that parenthetic definition Rees himself, helpfully although no doubt unwittingly, draws attention to something which makes this particular part of his thesis peculiarly implausible. Because crime is thus, by definition, a function of a legal system, what sorts of behaviour count as criminal is something which can, and in fact does, vary as between one system and another; and also, within the same system, from one time to another.[6] Some systems, such as those now of Britain and the United States, outlaw racial discrimination; whereas others, such as, most notoriously if not uniquely, that of South Africa, require it. Is it then a sign of psychological disorder to do in one country what it must by the same token be an indication of mental disease not to do in another?

The same applies with regard to temporal variations. Just possibly it might be conceded that, by liberalising previous criminal laws against male homosexual practices and abortion, the British Parliaments of 1964–1970 removed certain expressions of personality failure from the cognizance of the law; and certainly to say that all crimes are expressions of such failures is not to say that all such expressions are always crimes. But then it is surely almost impossible to believe that the creation of new economic offences by those and earlier Parliaments as steps towards the total Socialist goal of the Labour Party had the effect of uncovering other mental disorders formerly unrecognised.

Once the significance of this definitional point that crime is necessarily a function of a legal system is appreciated, it appears that the thesis that all crimes are as a matter of contingent fact symptoms of mental disease can be made credible in only two ways. It might be defended after the fashion described in the second paragraph of the present Section 3, by confounding it with a verbally similar non-contingent assertion. Alternatively it might be maintained in the contingent interpretation by appealing to further, supporting implausibilities. These in turn could also be of two kinds. In the first case the appeal would have to be to the altogether unbelievable contention that all offenders commit their offences precisely because these have been proscribed; while in the second case the assumption would be that all offences share some further characteristic, only contingently related to the fact that they happen to have been by some particular system forbidden. If all offenders in fact were as the first contention would maintain, or if that further characteristic were to be that of being madly imprudent, then perhaps we might proceed hopefully to suggest that offending does always happen to be a manifestation of some psychological disorder.

Consider, in illustration of the meaning of the first of these two alternatives, an exchange which occurred some years ago in a widely syndicated American women's page advice column. A correspondent wrote in to complain that her husband 'likes to break rules. . . . If there is a sign that says "No Smoking", he lights up at once. "Keep off the Grass" is an invitation. I have seen him step right over and stomp on the newly seeded lawn just for the devil of it. . . . Please tell me why he is like this, and what I can do about it.' She signs herself 'Married to a Nut'. She gets from the columnist Ann Landers the response: 'The "Nut" has emotional problems which go back many years. . . . He needs professional help.'[7]

It is doubtful whether anyone has ever believed that all or most crime is committed by this particular special sort of person. But the illusionary idea of a criminal type did once have famous protagonists, and it remains an idea which must in some form be required by anyone so misguided as to hope for a general theory of crime. Both the illusion and the aspiration are encouraged by the practice – common among both criminologists and the laity – of covertly and for no reason given discounting from consideration all those crimes which we ordinary law-abiding citizens might ourselves expect ever to commit. For by thus not attending to driving and parking offences, or to minor tax evasions, or to small thefts euphemistically called something else, crime is made to seem something which could only be committed by someone very unlike us. This practice of tacitly discounting certain categories of crime, and with it the suggestion that the criminal is a different sort of animal from ourselves, must sometimes have helped to support unsympathetic attitudes

towards (real) criminals and an inhumane treatment of them.
But it may also lead us to forget relevant but untrendy truths.
We may for instance by attending too closely to that factitiously
strange animal the (real) criminal, overlook, what from our own
experience of traffic controls we all know about, how sometimes
behaviour may be improved and bad habits broken by the
efficient enforcement of laws prescribing disagreeable penalties
for (criminal) offences.

The aspiration towards some general theory of crime, and
consequently the illusion, are also to some extent encouraged
by the mere existence of a field of study called criminology.
For if there are departments operating in our universities, then
there must of course be some corresponding subject-matter;
and wherever there is a recognised subject-matter – the argument might go on – there must be room for some comprehensive
general theory. But criminology is not that sort of field at all.
It is conspicuously not, that is to say, like biology or some
branch thereof. It can be salutary to insist, as indeed we have
just in a way been reminding ourselves, that the subject-matter
of the criminologist is entirely artificial. People do not – usually
– commit offences precisely because they are offences, and what
sorts of conduct are criminal is determined by what the particular system happens to proscribe. If you choose to study earthworms, then you have every reason to expect that your subjects
will have a great deal in common besides whatever it is which
makes them count as earthworms. But if you set up as a criminologist you will be surprisingly fortunate if you discover any
universal truths about crime and criminals save those which
follow necessarily from the initial definitions.

From a subject-matter so essentially artificial only the most
limited and qualified discoveries ought to be expected, although
these may be for all that both useful and disturbing. Criminology should thus perhaps be seen as a sort of miscellany of
Home Office studies. Indeed the usual tacit discountings
become in this context perfectly intelligible. For everyone can
see that traffic offences are really part of the province of the
Ministry of Transport; while pilfering from the office or the
works belongs, if it belongs to any ministry, to the Department
of Trade and Industry. It is finally just worth asking oneself
why no one thinks to investigate the causes and the cure of tort;
and why, if there are any university departments devoted to

tautology, it is tautology in a different sense, and with a different spelling.

★

4   The second of the two suggested ways in which the Rees thesis, in its contingent interpretation, might be defended was by urging 'that all offences share some further characteristic, only contingently related to the fact that they happen to have been by some particular system forbidden'; in particular, the characteristic of 'being madly imprudent'. The assumption that this is indeed so has an almost proverbial status. It is said that crime does not pay, or that honesty is the best (paying) policy. If any such claims were both true and visibly true one might, I suppose, maintain that all crime, or all dishonesty, or even all immorality in general, are so clearly and so crazily imprudent that criminal or dishonest or immoral actions can only be explained by reference to the agent's psychological disorder.

Certainly there actually are cases in which criminal behaviour does seem to be to a bizarre degree imprudent; just as there are, as we have just seen, real cases in which people perversely do things precisely and only because these things happen to be forbidden. Certainly too it is a mistake, often made by cynics and especially by the more brutal and corrupt sort of politician, to think that honesty never pays, or that what is the least honourable course is always politically the most advantageous. Take crime first. In the large sample which is the basis of his well-known study *Deliquency and Human Nature*, Dr D. H. Stott does find several such bizarre cases. But he proceeds – fortified, as I hope to show in Part III, by a misguiding philosophical doctrine – to write as if the rule were what an independent re-examination of his own recorded data will readily show to be the exception.

This disparity between conclusions and evidence is sharply pointed in a sentence which begins: 'The offender is so patently acting against his own interests.' This unqualified general contention is then supported, immediately after a semi-colon, by cautiously limited and thus inadequate claim: 'sometimes he does not even take the same precautions he would in crossing a road, even the most intelligent committing offences in a way which invites attention'. Later Stott repeats the unqualified general contention: 'Delinquency manifestly does not pay, persistence therein means, by ordinary standards, personal disaster apparently preferable to continuance in the existing situation.' Without some general assumption of this kind Stott could scarcely reach the equally unqualified final verdict: that 'delinquent breakdown is an escape from an emotional situation which, for the particular individual with the various conditionings of his background, becomes at least temporarily unbearable'.[8]

The short way to show the falsity of any universal and unqualified claim that crime, or delinquency, does not pay, is to refer again to variations between different times and different places. In a well-ordered society the rates of detection and conviction, and the relations between the penalties for and the attractions of whatever conduct is actually proscribed as criminal, may be such as to bring this saw as near to the truth as proverbial wisdom ever gets. Indeed that, as applied to a particular society, it should, is the most important traditional criterion for allowing that that society is well-ordered.

However all societies are not in this respect well-ordered: as a glance at the recent criminal statistics of for example either the United States, or Britain or Canada, will quickly confirm. So it cannot be universally true that on this account crime does not pay; much less that to commit an offence must always be a mark of ostensibly inexplicable imprudence; and much less still, as we shall be seeing in Part II, that extremes of either imprudence or eccentricity of motivation must in themselves negative accountability. And furthermore and finally, even if this premise in Stott's argument were fully supported by his own particular collection of data, we should still need to remind ourselves that, in anything less than a perfectly well-ordered society, the samples used in all such studies of convicted delinquents must be very relevantly unrepresentative. They cannot, that is to say, include the ones who got away.[9]

*

5   Consider next the parallel contention applying primarily not to crime but to immorality. Here we have not just a fragment of anonymous conventional wisdom but a thesis presented and defended by the most ancient and respectable authority.

For a version of this is dramatically the main proposition which Plato's Socrates undertakes to prove in *The Republic*. Three facts about the development of his argument are significant for us. First, it all relates to a perhaps authentically Socratic, and certainly characteristically Platonic, contention; the thesis customarily rendered 'No one willingly does wrong'. Second it involves what is, I believe, the earliest recorded attempt to show that vice is the expression of a kind of disease of the soul. Third it leads on to the surely originally Platonic demand for all power to a new class of experts, the elite order of Guardians, his true Philosopher Kings.

The Republic is supposed to be about justice, a sufficiently comprehensive virtue. The dialogue starts gently. But it comes vehemently alive with the intervention about half-way through Book I of the harsh debunker Thrasymachus. He maintains: that justice is not to the advantage of the just man himself, but to that of other people; that it is not a good for him, but for someone else; that it is – in the Greek words – not an *oikeion* [οἰκεῖον] but an *allotrion agathon* [ἀλλότριον ἀγαθόν]. (§343C) In a typical excess of cynicism Thrasymachus apparently takes it that this is so not merely often but always. Socrates in an equally typical excess of the opposite adopts the contrary position: 'I do not believe that injustice is more profitable than justice, not even if one leaves it free and does not hinder it from doing what it wants.' (§345A) In the rest of Book I Thrasymachus is put down. Then at the beginning of Book II Glaucon and Adeimantus return to the charge. The whole of the rest of *The Republic* is presented as the response of Socrates to this challenge.

It is here neither possible nor, fortunately, necessary to come to terms with this response fully and in detail. Our concern is only with the connections, some of which have been hinted already, between this thesis and the contentions that all crime, or all immorality or even all delinquency of whatever kind are expressions of mental disease. Thrasymachus plunges into the dialogue with what is presumably intended to be a definition of the word 'justice': " 'Listen then," he said, "for I say that justice is nothing else but the advantage of the stronger".' (S338c)[10]

We need to appreciate, as Plato's Socrates never did, that and why any such definition is and must be not merely wrong but diametrically wrong. It is wrong because to say that some

institution, or some course of conduct, is just is just not to say
that it is in the interest of the stronger party, or of the weaker
party, or of any other particular party; although of course on
almost any given occasion what happens to be just will happen
to be more or less in the interest of one or other party, or even
sometimes of all parties individually. But just as it is always a
further question to ask of what is allowed to have been prescribed by any authority whatever, 'Yes, but is it just and
right?'; so it is always a further question to ask, 'Yes, but is it
just and right?' of what is agreed to be in the interests of some
particular party.[11]

Worse still for any definition on Thrasymachean lines, the
whole point of an appeal to justice is precisely that it should
in this way be an appeal to some standard logically independent
of the interests of all particular contending parties. It would
be one thing for a Thrasymachus to snarl that there is no justice
if by this he meant that in some sense there is no such standard,
or that in a wicked world justice is never or very seldom done.
But it is quite another thing and, as has just been shown, diametrically wrong to assert that the word 'just' means the same
as the the expression 'advantageous to the stronger party'.
When the debunker says that what bad, powerful men really
mean when they claim that something is just, is just that it is
in their interests, what he really means is: not that this is either
what they mean nor yet the meaning of what they are saying;
but rather that this is what they would say if they were more
honest and less hypocritical. If the definition of Thrasymachus
were correct then there would be no hypocrisy here to unmask,
and no bunk to be debunked.

★

6   To show that 'justice' cannot be defined in terms of the
interests of any particular group or individual is not at all to
preclude the possibility of some non-contingent connection
between justice and the collective general interest. It is if anything to suggest the contrary. Conversely if you want to show
that justice is in the interests of each person and every party
individually it is not a bit of use to show that it is in the general
interests of the whole. For it is precisely the apparent lack of
correspondence between particular individual and wider col-

lective interests which first raised the pressing question whether to me individually it always is advantageous to act justly. The interlocutors of the Socrates of *The Republic* were therefore completely misguided when they accepted his insidiously persuasive methodological suggestion that they should inquire into the nature of justice by examining it first, writ large as it were, in an ideally just state: ' "So, if you agree, let us investigate its nature first in states, and only after this look at it in the individual too, searching for the likeness of the greater in the form of the less".' (§369A)

This method is relevantly unsound in two different ways. First it must be wrong, for the definitional reason indicated in Section 4 earlier, to look only to an ideally well-ordered society for your evidence to settle a question about the universal effects of just conduct upon the agent. For, once again, this sample is necessarily in a crucial way unrepresentative. That and why this is so Plato's Socrates fully appreciates. Indeed in his own way he stresses it: ' "That city, then is best ordered, isn't it, in which most people apply the terms 'mine' and 'not mine' to the same objects?".' (§462C)

What he apparently does not appreciate is the implication for his argument of the consequent unrepresentativeness. This failure is only one example of a systematic refusal throughout the whole dialogue adequately to distinguish contentions about what is the case from those about what ought to be. It can be no sort of reply to hard-bitten Thrasymachean assertions about how in this wicked world things actually are, to direct our attention to how, if we lived in an ideal world laid up in heaven. they would be. But of course Plato would not be Plato if he did not also have other arguments with which to try to show that these things must, perhaps in some profounder sense, stand here and now as they would stand there and then.

Second the method proposed must be wrong because it concentrates on the collective, whereas what is chiefly in dispute is whether what very well may hold – what does perhaps even hold necessarily – of the collective does also hold of the individual. The force of this objection can be brought out by referring back to an argument put by Socrates in Book I much earlier. Socrates there asks Thrasymachus: ' "Would you think that a state, or an army, or a gang of thieves, or bandits, or any other group, which attempts to carry out unjust actions collectively would be able to accomplish anything if they treated one another unjustly?".' (§351) Obviously not, it is agreed. Taking a modern illustration, one might ask rhetorically whether Germany could have begun to be the global menace which it was had it not been for the integrity and devotion of its Prussian-trained civil service, the soldierly virtues and above all the readiness for sacrifice of the members of its armed forces.

Socrates draws the moral that injustice is essentially disruptive, and must tend to make any group in which it is prevalent ineffective to achieve any common purpose: ' "Is it not, therefore, apparent that its force is such, wherever it is found, whether in a state or in a family or in an army or whatever else, as to render it incapable through conflict and faction of internal co-operation . . . ? Isn't that so?".' (§§351E–352A) The final move in this argument is a quick, fatal step from the collective to the individual: ' "And in the individual too, I imagine, it will produce all these effects which it is its nature to produce. It will in the first place make him through his internal conflict and disintegration incapable of action, and then an enemy to himself and to the just. Is it not so?".' (§352A)

To this startling conclusion Plato scripts the now chastened Thrasymachus to reply meekly, 'Yes.' No doubt the premises upon which Socrates relies here, though embodying an important truth, require much qualification. But our present concern is not with the truth of either premises or conclusion. Rather it is to underline the point that it cannot be sound in any such disputed case to argue, from what may or may not be true premises about the group, directly to conclusions about the individual. That that Prussian integrity and devotion, that soldierly virtue and readiness for sacrifice, made for formidable German military power, has no tendency to show that these qualities were always advantageous to those who displayed them. In what, had that been so, one might again ask rhetorically, would their actual sacrifices then have consisted?

*

7   Now neither justice, nor what is meant by the original Greek word, is the whole of virtue. But they certainly are parts, and large parts. Equally certainly to show that there is no necessary connection between an action's being just and its

being in the interests of the man who performs it, is not to show that there is not a contingent coincidence between justice and individual self-interest. Rather, the relevance of the last four paragraphs of the previous Section 6 is that they suggest that, if there really is any such universal coincidence, this contingent coincidence must be regarded as a providential fact. Yet that there is, is implied by claims that all delinquencies, or at any rate all delinquencies which constitute defections from duty, are expressions of mental disease. For to be in any way diseased must surely be in itself, and apart from any offsetting special circumstances; against any interests. It ought to strike us as a very remarkable piece of prevenient adaptation of human nature to society if all defections from the requirements of the common good happen also to be against the individual interests of the defector.

Once this providential assumption is clearly revealed as such, and squarely faced, it appears to go against much of our immediate experience. It is hard to understand how we could have come to develop, and frequently to contrast, the two separate concepts of morality and of prudence had not their apparent dictates been often in conflict. The existence too of penal institutions is a poor advertisement for either the visibility or the completeness of the correlation assumed. For where, in those many cases where what is criminal is also immoral, would be the need for legally proscribing the offence, and trying to catch the offender and to penalise him artificially, if it were obvious that he was in any case going to suffer some sufficient natural penalty? Again where would be the urgency of delineating formidable deterrent schemes of a postulated future life if to do justice always is, and can be shown to be, in the this-worldly interests of all concerned? There is no need to call in a new world to redress the balance of the old except in so far as that balance is, or at least seems to be, upset.

So if the providential assumption is to be found to be correct, it will be by showing to our surprise that the real situation is radically different from the apparent. One way to do this would be by establishing the Rees thesis. For this presupposes, and hence also entails, the providential assumption. An elegant way to bring out that these logical relations do obtain is to work with Plato. For it was precisely in order to establish what I have been labelling the providential assumption that Plato developed his case for a version of the Rees thesis.

What follows from such a claim that delinquency is an expression of mental disease all depends, or all partly depends, on what you mean by 'mental disease'. Equally certainly the word 'disease', and nowadays the expression 'mental disease', may be employed to carry very little meaning. Sometimes to say 'It's a disease' or 'It's a mental disease' amounts to little more than a verbal shrug of disapproval. Yet even in such minimal cases the choice of these words is bound to carry nuances different from those of saying either, moralistically, 'This is a wicked affair' or, more non-committally, 'This is a bad business'. Sometimes again, there is just a little more to it than that, although only a little. The writer on the *Worthies of Warwickshire* cited in Sir James Murray's *Oxford English Dictionary* deploring that 'Bad Latin was a catching disease in that age' was, we may assume, employing the expression 'catching disease' to make three lighthearted points. First this bad Latin is a bad show. Second the habits involved are communicated to others by close contacts with those in whom such lamentable habits are already established. Third this at its own level constitutes a crisis situation.

But these are derivative – not to say degenerate – uses. They can be appreciated only on the basis of an understanding of the full and primary meaning. They have to be mentioned in passing because they are there; and to emphasise by contrast that our concern is with that richer significance, in which the application of the term carries implications which matter. When Plato contends that vice is a sort of psychological disease he is not just uttering a verbal shudder. Nor is he latching on to a merely peripheral similarity between vices and physical diseases – like the fact that both may sometimes be spread by close contacts. He is, rather, insisting that there are crucial and central similarities. That is what gives profundity to his contention, and what makes it perennially challenging and important. His case is quite opposite to that in which Shakespeare's Falstaff confesses to disease only to confess that he was not diseased. There the Lord Chief Justice says: ' "I think you are fallen into the disease; for you hear not what I say to you".' Falstaff replies: ' "Very well, my lord, very well: rather, and it please you, it is the disease of not listening, the malady of not marking, that I am troubled withal".' (*Henry IV*, Part II, Act I, Sc. 2.)

The same holds true of other spokesmen for the ideas of mental health and mental illness, including many who would give short shrift to the Rees thesis. It was to what he believed to be central and fundamental similarities that Philippe Pinel appealed when he maintained, in words quoted among the mottoes of this essay: 'The mentally ill, far from being guilty persons who merit punishment, are sick people whose miserable state deserves all the consideration due to suffering humanity.' The British Royal Commission on the Law Relating to Mental Illness and Mental Deficiency (reporting in 1957) were in the same tradition when with satisfaction they asserted: 'The general public now know more about mental illness and are more sympathetic to people suffering from it than ever before.'[12]

Both passages emphasise two fundamental resemblances between disease, in the primary physical sense, and what is to be called mental disease: that in both cases something is wrong with the patient which is bad for him; and that the patient, as is appropriately suggested by that choice of word, is with respect to this something victim rather than agent. The same emphases are prominent in the conclusions of Plato's Socrates. To appreciate what is going on it is necessary to notice certain difficulties of translation. The Greek word which always is and can scarcely not be translated as 'soul' is *psyche* (ψυχή); from which English gets the 'psych' part of such words as 'psychiatry', 'psychoanalysis', 'psychosomatic' and 'psychological'. It is thus etymologically apt when Plato writes about an illness or disorder of this ψυχή for us to render him as discussing psychological disease. This is indeed, I think, as near as contemporary English can get to the flavour of the original Greek. For the word 'soul' – like for instance the word 'vouchsafe' – has now acquired peculiarly clerical associations; and these seem to have the effect of neutralising the strongly medical implications of the word 'disease'. Perhaps this is why Plato has not until very recently been recognised as the first parent of the Rees thesis.

★

8   Having, he thinks, established that an ideally just state would be an hierarchical structure of three classes or castes, and that its justice would consist in everyone's sticking to his own job and his own proper place in the hierarchy, Plato's

Socrates develops a parallel consideration of justice in the individual – justice writ small, as it were. He argues that every
individual soul is also constituted of three elements, corresponding to the three classes or castes of *The Republic*. His immediate
conclusion is that justice in the individual is for each of these
elements to do its own job, to fulfil its proper function in the
psychological hierarchy: 'We must remember, then, that each
of us too in whom each of his internal elements does its own
work will be a just man and one doing his own job.' (§441D–E)

It is after this that he develops and presses the analogy
between the health of the body and the health of the soul. The
first emphasis is on the fulfilment of natural functions, and also
on harmonious integration and co-ordination; two further
features which he takes to be essential to health, but which
have not so far been mentioned in our discussion. The contention is that justice and injustice 'are in the soul what health
and disease are in the body; there is no difference'. For 'to
produce health is to establish the elements in the soul in the
natural relations of domination and subjection, while to cause
disease is to bring it about that one rules or is ruled by another
contrary to nature'. (§444C–D)

There are two points to be made here. First it is no accident
that Plato's phrasing here suggests that, typically, both sorts of
health are produced by the controlling activity of someone else.
It is one of the basic and distinctive ideas of *The Republic* that
all power should be given to specially trained experts. They
alone can secure both health in the state, and health and justice
in the souls of its citizens; and to the treatments of these new
experts, qualified by their recondite knowledge of the Platonic
Forms or Ideas, we should surrender ourselves as absolutely
as patients to a trusted doctor. Although this suggestion that
the proper response is treatment by a qualified expert could
scarcely be said to be part of the meaning of the word 'disease',
it certainly is one which those who press the analogy between
two sorts of health always want to make. Thus for instance the
very first sentence of the 1957 Report of the Royal Commission
aforementioned reads: 'Disorders of the mind are illnesses which
need medical treatment.' It is again this same initially innocu-
ous suggestion to which the political scientist H. D. Lasswell
gives a fully Platonic development in a remarkable contribution
to *Psychiatry* for 1938: 'Must the psychiatrist, then, unseat the

king and actualize in the realm of fact the "philosopher-king" of Plato's imagination? . . . if sufficiently secure in his knowledge of himself and his field, he may dare where others dared and lost before.'[13]

If the phrases 'it is no accident that' and 'all power to' call to mind Soviet political commentators and Leninist slogans, that is fitting. For Russell was entirely right when he remarked, after returning from a private tour of Lenin's Russia in 1920, in his middle and less Communist-inclined years: 'Far closer than any actual historical parallel is the parallel of Plato's *Republic*.'[14] The treatments which his Guardian doctors might need to employ could be similarly drastic. No one could complain that for Plato the thesis that all delinquency is an expression of psychological disease constituted 'A Mollycoddler's Charter'. For he, like F. H. Bradley in the last century, construed his bio-medical analogies as a Guardian's licence to practise 'social surgery'.[15]

The second and more fundamental point is that Plato's soul, though essentially incorporeal, was also supposed to be a substance; something, that is, which could significantly be said to exist separately. Whereas for us to say that someone has a third-rate, or a convoluted or an incisive mind is simply to say in a different idiom something about his qualities and inclinations; for Plato the soul, being a substance, must be more like the lost bone than the lost temper of the dog in chapter ix of *Through the Looking-Glass*. While the doctor attends the body, the soul-doctor attends the not-body. But Plato also identifies the (more or less) rational agent with the soul: we are our souls. So whatever can be said to be wrong in a person, as a person, can now easily be thought of as a disorder of a not-organ; and hence, obviously, as a medical matter.[16]

Having arrived by such routes at the position that unjust conduct must be a manifestation of psychological disorder, Plato is easily able to show that his desired conclusion constitutes a corollary. His Socrates says: ' "And now at last, it seems, it remains for us to inquire whether it is profitable to do justice and to engage in splendid activities and to be a just man, regardless of whether one is known to be such or not; or whether it is profitable to do injustice and to be unjust, always providing that you escape punishment and are not improved by chastisement".'

The answer for anyone who has both understood and accepted what has gone before, is obvious. So the final move can be given to Glaucon; who has, I am afraid, by now become the most ventriloqual of what are in less elevated contexts called feed-men: ' "But, Socrates, it seems to me that our inquiry now becomes ridiculous. Are we – while it is admitted that with a ruined bodily constitution, even when you have got all the food and drink in the world and all the wealth and power, life is not worth living – are we going to ask whether, even when you can do whatever you like except what will release you from corruption and injustice and possess you of justice and excellence, life will be worth living with the very nature of that by which we live disordered and corrupted? For the two things have been shown to be as we have described them." ' (§445A–B)

★

9   But they are not. For though the patient with a ruined physical constitution can be expected at least to be tempted to feel that his life is on that account not worth living, the same is surely not true of the parallel case of the morally corrupt agent. No doubt he ought to feel that his moral corruption makes his life not worth living. But to say this is a very different thing from saying that he actually and always in fact does. Indeed if he did he would presumably be beginning to take some first steps upon the uphill path of his own reformation. But that case, though it does occur, is unhappily not the only case.

Since the conclusion is false we have to ask what went wrong to get us there. The answer clearly is that the source of the trouble was the equation of the doing of injustice with the suffering of a psychological disease. For if unjust behaviour really were symptomatic of psychological disease, in as near as makes no matter the same sense of 'disease' as that in which diphtheria and pneumonia are said to be diseases, then the unjust man would be with respect to his unjust behaviour not an agent but a victim. Which seems to involve two things. First his disease – including its natural but not its artificial consequences – must be not just generally in some way a bad thing but particularly and in itself for him and in his eyes a bad thing. Second although it may be partly or wholly a consequence of his own actions it must not be something which he is now able to escape immediately and at will.

This offers a welcome occasion to refer to Samuel Butler's famous fantasy *Erewhon*. The points can be brought out very clearly in considering his account in chapter 10 of Erewhonian 'Current Opinions'. For

> in that country if a man falls into ill health, or catches any disorder, or fails bodily in any way before he is seventy years old, he is tried before a jury of his countrymen, and if convicted is held up to public scorn and sentenced more or less severely as the case may be . . . But if a man forges a cheque, or sets his house on fire, or robs with violence from the person, or does any other such things as are criminal in our own country, he is either taken to a hospital and most carefully tended at the public expense, or, if he is in good circumstances, he lets it be known to all his friends that he is suffering from a severe fit of immorality, just as we do when we are ill, and they come to visit him with great solicitude, and inquire with interest how it all came about, what symptoms first showed themselves, and so forth. . . .

Butler presents his paradox well. It need be no surprise that among his admirers was the young George Bernard Shaw. Crime and immorality among the Erewhonians, Butler goes on, are therefore dealt with by 'a class of men trained in soul-craft, whom they call straighteners, as nearly as I can translate a word, which literally means "one who bends back the crooked". These men practise much as medical men in England. . . . They are treated with the same unreserve, and obeyed as readily, as our own doctors – that is to say on the whole sufficiently – because people know that it is to their interest to get well as soon as they can, and that they will not be scouted as they would be if their bodies were out of order, even though they may have to undergo a very painful course of treatment.'

The second and definitive edition of *Erewhon* was first published in 1901. It is therefore a remarkable example of life imitating art that in 1924 the American Orthopsychiatric Association was founded with the object of bringing together 'representatives of the neuropsychiatric or medical view of crime'. (Our English 'ortho' comes from a Greek root meaning straight.) But the point which has to be made here is that the complete reversal presented by Butler is not intelligible. There is of course no difficulty about the idea that people might be criminally arraigned for falling sick. The suggestion is only morally, not logically, scandalous. Indeed in English criminal law 'there are now offences (known as offences of "strict liability") where it is not necessary for conviction to show that the accused either intentionally did what the law forbids or could have avoided doing it by use of care; selling liquor to an intoxicated person, possessing an altered passport, selling adulterated milk are examples. . . .'[17]

Nor further is it at all unintelligible that 'if a man forges a cheque, or sets his house on fire, or robs with violence from the person, or does any other such things as are criminal in our own country' he might be 'taken to a hospital and most carefully tended at the public expense'. Nor again should it even be surprising that some of the treatments administered in such institutions might be more beastly and more obnoxious to those who suffer them than most penalties now legally inflicted in most prisons. It is after all partly, although – as I shall urge later – not mainly, because a day in the Serbsky Institute for Forensic Psychiatry can be even more awful than *A Day in the Life of Ivan Denisovitch* that the KGB has developed the practice of incarcerating intractable dissidents in such 'mental hospitals'. Even in the United States there is on the record a statement, from one who had also served terms in the prisons of Florida, Georgia, Virginia and Maryland, that he would prefer a year in any one of these – not excluding the chain-gangs – to six months in St Elizabeth's Hospital in the District of Columbia.[18] What is perhaps a little, if only a little, more surprising in Butler is the failure of either nerve or imagination manifested in listing among the Erewhonian orthopsychiatric treatments only traditionally penal measures – 'close confinement for weeks. . . . a flogging once a week, and a diet of bread and water for two or three months together'.

The actual incoherence in Butler's account constitutes a dramatic weakness. It is of a kind which might be expected to attract the attention of even the most purely literary critic.[19] The incoherence is that Butler does not suggest, and surely could not have suggested, any intelligible motivation to account for the behaviour of Erewhonians who put themselves into the hands of their straighteners when their offences have not been, and are not perhaps likely to be, detected. Take Mr Nosnibor, the stockbroker, who had been sailing rather close to the wind: 'He had unfortunately made light of it and pooh-poohed the ailment, until circumstances eventually presented themselves which enabled him to cheat upon a very considerable scale . . . he seized the opportunity, and became aware, when it was too late, that he must be seriously out of order.'

Certainly cheating is a bad business – if not always perhaps bad business. Certainly there is something wrong with a cheat, at least in the sense that he ought to be other than he is. But this gives us still no reason why Mr Nosnibor should have come to see his cheating as bad for him, and be acting accordingly by sending voluntarily 'for one of the most celebrated straighteners of the kingdom'. Since presumably he wants the money which he has been successfully acquiring by cheating, his cheating seems so far to have been a very good thing for him. Certainly no other explanation has been offered as to why he began to cheat in the first instance – nor yet for that matter to stockbroke. And it has not even been claimed that criminal behaviour is never under the subject's control. Compare the case from the advice column of Ann Landers (quoted at page 7 above). Although the advice was that the husband had 'emotional problems' and needed 'professional help', no one had said anything to show that his tiresome and destructive behaviour was not fully under his control; and the fact that the heartcry came from the wife and not the husband strongly suggested that any immediate problems were primarily problems for her not problems for him.

The problem therefore for Butler is that he is trying to represent dramatically a total reversal as between sickness roles and delinquency roles; but to do this while still assuming that the general facts about human nature and social life are in the relevant and crucial respects as they have been traditionally believed to be. But the practice of sending spontaneously for the straightener in cases such as that of Mr Nosnibor could be made intelligible only if all delinquents really are, in the sense indicated at the beginning of this present Section 9, victims and not agents of their delinquencies. This, even if it were true, would certainly be contrary to the assumption.

It would furthermore be equally fatal to Butler's inherently impossible project to provide that in a new *Erewhon* everyone

who did not spontaneously ask for the orthopsychiatric treatment he was supposed to need would be forced to have it anyway. It would not help, that is, for Butler to take a leaf out of
the book of the Massachussetts judge who recently put a confessed and convicted murderess on probation for ten years 'with
the stipulation that she voluntarily committed herself to the
Massachussetts Mental Health Center for treatment'.[20] For,
however obliquely, any such move must underline what is
for this project the ruinous difference: between on the one
hand those typical cases of delinquency in which the supposed
victims have to be artificially induced to accept treatments
promising relief; and on the other hand those cases typical of
physical disease in which actual sufferers do spontaneously
summon – or nowadays themselves dance attendance on – their
body-doctors.

★

10   This crucial difference did not of course escape Plato,
although sometimes it does seem to be escaping some of his
unwitting successors. But to him it appeared not as falsifying
the cherished claim that delinquencies are the expressions of
the disease of the soul, but instead as strengthening the still
more cherished consequence that all delinquents should either
submit themselves or be forcibly submitted to a regimen prescribed by those first specialist straighteners, the Guardians.
For Plato was already committed to a doctrine, developed in
earlier dialogues, which implied that any unwillingness to
submit to such treatments, any protests against compulsory
psychiatric medications, could spring only from a tragic ignorance on the part of the patients of the ruinously diseased
condition of their souls. Such ignorant objections must, in the
interests of the patients as much as of everyone else, be firmly
overridden by the qualified authorities.

The doctrine from which he generates these consequences
is customarily rendered: 'No one willingly does wrong.' This
traditional epitome is misleading: it suppresses the fact that
the word translated as 'does wrong' – ἁμαρτάνει [read hamar-
tanei] – still carries its original meaning of 'fails', or 'misses the
mark'; and it puts the emphasis on the will, whereas Plato
himself stressed the intellect. His general line was: since all
men always and necessarily do whatever seems good to them,

when they do what is in truth bad, then it can only be because they have mistaken appearance for reality. Since it was also assumed that whatever is good is also good for you, your characteristic and habitual evildoing must manifest gross failure on your part to appreciate your own interests; and this cannot but be diagnosed as a psychological disorder. What delinquency essentially consists in, Plato holds, is the failure of the elements of the soul to perform their functions harmoniously. This is a failure strictly parallel to that failure of bodily organs to perform their functions harmoniously which, Plato takes it, is physical disease.[21]

Our discussion of Plato's development of conceptions of mental health and mental disease has now served its purpose.[22] This purpose is subordinate to the main aim of the whole of Part I, which has been to present an outline of the fundamental ideas, their implications and their connections. Such an outline may serve as a sketchmap to save us from getting lost in the all-encircling mists of a climate of opinion. It is a moment to quote Nietzsche: 'The Greeks are like genius, simple. That is why they are immortal teachers.'

II Disease and Mental Disease

1   One main outcome of Part I should be a realisation of the dependence of the derivative notions of mental health and mental disease upon the prior notions of (physical) health and (physical) disease. If this dependence were merely historical and etymological it would be of little present concern. To urge that the true and proper meaning of all expressions as now employed must be determined by either the ultimate etymology or the original English senses of the words involved is unsound and tiresome. But it is both correct and important to insist that, if a large part of the point of applying the descriptions 'mental health' and 'mental disease' is to imply that most if not quite all which is involved in (physical) health and (physical) disease is involved in these further cases also, then any attempt to elucidate the former should begin from some preliminary examination of the latter.

This modest methodological claim may appear trite and obvious. But triteness and obviousness are essentially relative to time and place and person. For it is most remarkable how little attention seems to be paid in the now abundant literature on the nature and criteria of mental health and mental disease to the similarities and dissimilarities between these and their physical analogues. Indeed the present essay will, I believe, be sufficiently justified if it succeeds in persuading some future contributors to this literature to proceed in this now obviously sound way.

Consider as a first example Dr Marie Jahoda's *Current Concepts of Positive Mental Health*. This is an American work. It was sponsored by the 'Joint Commission on Mental Illness and Health, as part of a national mental health survey that will culminate in a final report containing findings and recommendations for a national mental health program'. This whole enterprise achieved a most authoritative vindication when only five years later on 5 February 1963 President Kennedy issued his Message to the Congress on 'Mental Health and Mental Retardation'. Dr Jahoda begins: 'There is hardly a term in current psychological thoughts as vague, elusive, and ambiguous as the term "mental health". . . . The purpose of this review is to clarify a variety of efforts to give meaning to this vague notion.' She proceeds to classify and to discuss a great many such efforts. Yet, almost incredibly, she never once develops any comparisons between mental health as so conceived and physical health; and neither, it seems, did any of the authorities from whom she quotes. What is revealed is, as her introductory remarks suggest, a conceptual shambles. But she herself concludes, quite inappropriately, with the familiar mandatory appeal for more (expensive) empirical research: 'a slow and costly' striving 'for more and better knowledge about the conditions conducive to mental health'.[23]

The nearest which anyone in this whole book gets to what should be the fundamental comparison is a hint in a dissenting – perhaps in this context one should say grumbling – Appendix. This nearest is still not very near. But Dr Walter Barton does put as the 'Viewpoint of a Clinician' what he qualifies, but does not express, as a conceptual insight: 'Conceptually, it is difficult to see how a national program . . . can be operated' except in as much as 'illness is the point of departure and health is the goal.'[24] This negatively constructive emphasis contrasts with the hankering felt by Dr Jahoda herself, by the Staff Director of the Joint Commission, and by most of Dr Jahoda's quoted authorities, for some robustly North American accentuation of the positive. Thus the Staff Director writes in his prefatory 'Staff Review' of 'interest in mental health, as a positive force . . . to be made conceptually clear and practically useful'. He notes that the 'behavioural scientists who have joined the mental health team and are making increasingly important contributions to the mental health movement have expressed dissatisfaction with a primary focus on "sick behaviour" '.[25] Very significantly there is even talk, here and elsewhere, of 'the mental health ideology'. Dr Jahoda's own chosen title *Current Concepts of Positive Mental Health* is also entirely apt to the contributions she does actually find herself examining.[26]

*

2   A second illustration, which again has some representative status, is provided by a Report of the Scientific Committee of the World Federation for Mental Health. Entitled 'Mental Health and Value Systems', it appeared with another on 'Identity' as a pair of *Cross-Cultural Studies in Mental Health*, published in a single volume edited by Dr Kenneth Soddy. Dr Soddy is an Englishman, Scientific Director of the Federation, and also Secretary of the Scientific Committee. The volume was issued in 1961 as 'A World Mental Health Year Publication'.

The Report begins by noticing 'that mental health is increasingly becoming a value, in a similar sense to the modern concept of bodily health'. It takes this observation as setting its own task: 'If this be truly an emerging concept, then it is time to consider the relationship between mental health and the established value systems of people.'[27] Here the question should arise whether there is or has been a corresponding cross-cultural problem about physical health; and, if not, or even if so, what it is about mental health which makes the difference.

The nearest which the Report comes to recognising and answering this question is in considering 'the acceptances of mental health concepts' and 'the resistances' thereto. 'Here', it says, 'an interesting comparison can be made with the acceptance of the notion of physical health.' Indeed it can be. But it is not made here. Instead the Report continues: 'The latter has not always been regarded as a "good object" but, although the operative description of physical health may be scarcely less vague than that of mental health, in recent years and in many parts of the world, physical health has become increasingly recognised as important and valuable. . . . If the concept of physical health as a "good object" has been acceptable only with difficulty, that of mental health is likely to provoke even greater resistances.'[28]

No reason whatsoever is offered why we should accept the incredible protasis. No hint is given of any peculiar interpretation in which it might possibly be true. That distinguished signatories could bring themselves to assert, as a fact requiring no evidential support, that physical health has only recently come to be regarded as a good thing, constitutes a noteworthy indication of how some people – and not only rather

young people – are able to believe anything about the dark
days before they were born. An age which no longer reads
the Bible certainly cannot remember its Apocrypha: 'Health
and good estate of body are above all gold.' (*Ecclesiasticus*,
XXX 15)

Even if we were to accept the bold assertion about struggles
for the acceptance of physical health as a good thing we still
need, but are not given, a reason why mental health should
be expected to encounter not the same but 'even greater
resistances'. The Report thus fails to make anything but a
memorable nonsense of its only explicit attempt to compare
mental with physical health. Where a crucial difference might
have been revealed the opening gap is covered over with an
enormous counter-factual assumption.

If you do not start right, with a faithful comparison between
proposed notions of mental health and the original physical
paradigm, you cannot hope to bring out clearly why these
former seem to be beset by ideological disputes and cross-
cultural conflicts of a kind which scarcely afflict the latter at
all. Certainly ideology is sometimes relevant to the practice
of physical medicine. A Jehovah's Witness for instance may not
accept a blood transfusion. A hard-line Roman Catholic doctor
will not in any circumstances perform an abortion. But, if
we waive at this stage the question whether the conditions for
which a secular doctor would be likely to prescribe these
treatments could be called strictly disease, these are disagreements not about diagnoses but about what it is permissible
to do about conditions of which the diagnoses may be taken
as agreed. Such disagreements are not therefore of the same
kind as those with which Dr Jahoda is concerned. For these
do not spring, as those do, from differences with regard to the
correct criteria for the application of the diagnostic expressions
'mental health' and 'mental disease'.

To see why mental health as conceived by Dr Jahoda is an
inherently disputatious notion, in a way in which physical
health is not, consider the first paragraph of her statement of
the 'Purpose and Scope' of her study: 'The purpose of this
review is to clarify a variety of efforts to give meaning to this
vague notion. In doing so we shall have to examine the assumptions about the nature of man and society underlying such
efforts by making explicit some of their implications and con-

sequences. This should lead first to a description of various types of human behaviour called mentally healthy and second to a discussion of mental health concepts suggested in the literature.'[29]

No mere body doctor needs to examine 'assumptions about the nature of man and society' before he can decide whether the man in front of him is or is not physically fit. The crux lies in the emphasis in the following sentence on behaviour. If 'mental health' is to be officially defined, as Dr Jahoda here suggests, in terms of what people actually do do, rather than in terms of what they are capable of doing, then the notion as so defined becomes liable to be involved in every dispute about ideals and actions. By the same token it must thereby lose some of its logical connections with the concept of physical health. For it is notorious that a man may be physically fit but a scoundrel, sick yet a saint. So if the analogy between mental and physical health is to be preserved here, then we must provide for the parallel possibility of saying for instance that whereas St Francis of Assisi suffered from various mental diseases 'Scarface' Al Capone enjoyed the rudest of rude mental health.

The Report to the World Federation is even more explicit about the ideologically committed character of its concepts of mental health; although, as we have just seen, by making a truly heroic assumption the authors then conceal from themselves the size of the gap which is thus opened between mental and physical health. They start from two principles: 'That there can be different degrees of mental health; and that mental health is associated with . . . the prevailing religion or ideology of the community concerned.' Curiously, they fail to remark the apparent although not perhaps ultimate inconsistency of this sort of cultural relativism with their own absolute insistence later 'that the members of a group of individuals who remain contented while they are in an inferior position in society fail to satisfy some of the important criteria of mental health. We would like also to question the state of mental health of the "superior" group in that society.' The Reporters also display at this point the tendency, common in 'the mental health movement' and among 'the mental health team', to pack all possible goods into one single, all-embracing, conflict-conceal-ing ideal; which for them makes 'mental health' a revamped

and scientistic substitute for the 'summum bonum' of an
older generation of philosophers.[30]

★

3   A third example of failure fully to come to terms with
the physical paradigm is provided by two chapters in Lady
Wootton's *Social Science and Social Pathology*. These are for two
reasons of especial interest to us. First she also is approaching
notions of mental disease from a primary concern with delinquency. Second she does turn her eyes to the physical paradigm
much more frequently than others do. Thus in the first of these
two chapters, 'Social Pathology and the Concepts of Mental
Health and Mental Illness', she starts by noticing how 'in the
course of a couple of centuries some wheels have come nearly
full circle . . . instead of treating lunatics as criminals, we now
regard many criminals as lunatics, or at any rate as mentally
disordered'.[31]

She proceeds to pick out as 'underlying the prevailing
contemporary views . . . a series of closely related propositions'.
The first is that

> mental health and its correlative, mental illness, are objec-
> tive in the sense that they are more than an expression either
> of the tastes and value-judgements of psychiatrists, or of the
> cultural norms of a particular society: mental health is to be
> regarded as closely analogous to, and no less 'real' than, its
> physical counterpart. Second, it is presumed to be possible
> . . . to diagnose these objective conditions . . . by criteria
> which are independent of any anti-social behaviour on the
> part of those who suffer from them; so that anti-social per-
> sons can be divided into the two classes of those who are men-
> tally disordered, and those who are not thus handicapped.

The second of these is presumably a consequence of the first,
provided only that the necessary possibility is taken to be
sometimes theoretical and not always practical. The distinction to which it refers, between criteria which are or are not
independent, relates to that developed in Section 3 of Part I,
between logically necessary and logically contingent interpretations. But what Lady Wootton presents as a corollary of this
second assumption, is not. For, as has surely been made clear
by later sections of that part, it is although rash perfectly

coherent to maintain a version of the extreme Rees thesis in a contingent and consequently providential interpretation. You could, that is to say, without contradiction assert that all delinquencies, as identified by one set of appropriate criteria, are as a matter of fact expressions of mental diseases, as identified by another and altogether different set of appropriate criteria. In the remainder of this chapter Lady Wootton examines a large number of suggested definitions of 'mental health' and 'mental disease'. She concludes that these one and all fail to justify the first of the series of closely related assumptions which she distinguished at the beginning.

In the next chapter she considers 'Mental Disorder and Criminal Responsibility'. It is here that her readiness to pursue analogies with the physical paradigm is most evident and most salutary. She notices for instance that we do not allow without further argument that every disease must fully excuse any conduct whatever in its subject. Indeed that a man is suffering from such and such a physical disease is sometimes irrelevant to, sometimes excuses and sometimes compounds his offence. So in so far as the analogy between the mental and the physical holds we should expect the same to apply with mental disease. For example: the fact that I do suffer terribly from a duodenal ulcer must surely excuse a general shortness of temper; but it can scarcely be allowed to expunge my offence in implementing some elaborately spiteful premeditated scheme. Again the fact that you are afflicted with a disease of the eyes which disables you from judging speeds and distances does nothing to extenuate your guilt in killing a man in a car crash. On the contrary: that you knew of this disability makes it altogether inexcusable to have been driving a car at all. Finally, to quote one of Lady Wootton's own happily shrewd questions, 'Why should we accept a plea of diminished responsibility for the unlawful revenges of the deluded against their imaginary persecutors, but not for similar actions perpetrated against real enemies by rational persons, if both parties alike recognize what they do as wrong?'[33]

We must however challenge the astonishing contention made at the very beginning of this second chapter. She writes: 'If mental health and ill-health cannot be defined in objective scientific terms that are free of subjective moral judgements, it follows that we have no reliable criterion by which to distinguish the sick from the healthy mind. The road is then wide open for those who wish to classify all forms of anti-social, or at least criminal, behaviour as symptoms of mental disorder.'[34]

What is most immediately astonishing about this is the conclusion that the collapse of all attempts to develop a suitably objective distinction between mental health and mental disease must clear the way for assertions that all behaviour of some particular disfavoured sort is in fact a symptom of mental disorder. For it is clear that all concerned are continuing to assume that the truth of any such assertion would license certain inferences about the behaviour in question, inferences which are only warranted if and in so far as it does in some or indeed in most important respects actually resemble the symptoms of a typical physical disorder. But we certainly are not entitled to claim that something is the case regardless of whether or not there are any good grounds for maintaining that this is in fact so. If all attempts to develop a suitably objective distinction parallel to the distinction between physical health and physical disease have indeed collapsed, then the true moral is not that we are entitled to assert of anything we choose that it is always a symptom of mental disorder. It is rather that it is not legitimate to try to employ the expression 'mental disease' in any sense presupposing the subsistence of a strong and extensive analogy between such mental disease and physical disease.

Although, as we have just this moment seen, this is not what Lady Wootton actually says here, it is nevertheless a position which she might be content to hold. For she is going on to urge that we are and, she seems inclined to think, should be moving towards 'abandoning the concept of responsibility'; an abandonment which would involve 'a shift of emphasis in the treatment of offenders away from considerations of guilt and towards choice of whatever course of action appeared most likely to be effective as a cure in any particular case'.[35] But, to the extent that we give up asking questions about guilt, we lose the occasions to ask whether the behaviour under discussion may be excused as the symptom of mental disease. Hence we shall have no need, at least in this context, for that concept of mental disease which she holds 'cannot be defined in objective scientific terms'.

Lady Wootton makes this interesting and unusual position

possible by distinguishing two different contentions; both of which, she thinks, are commonly put forward without discrimination. She begins by quoting a multiply obnoxious manifesto from the *Journal of Mental Science*. Its author speaks of the 'concepts of responsibility and punishment popular in legal and psychiatric practice' as 'theological and metaphysical anachronisms' fit only for the decadent 'amusement of the religious and others of that kidney'. All that really matters in any case of delinquency is that 'appropriate action may be decided upon. Questions of "mad" or "bad", with their value-judgements and emotional loadings, do not arise. We are confronted with a person who has committed some action that is abnormal, by its infrequency of occurrence, and that has brought its doer into conflict with his fellows; we have to decide how to obviate or minimise repetition of such conflict, for the good of all concerned.'[36]

She also quotes Dr Bernard Glueck, the Supervising Psychiatrist of Sing Sing. He starts by wondering whether 'present psychiatric knowledge' is not already sufficient to undermine the idea of freewill. He goes on to suggest that 'the question of responsibility would not have to be raised, if the concept of management of the anti-social individual were changed from that of punishment as the main instrument of control, to a concept of the anti-social individual as a sick person, in need of treatment rather than punishment'. About this Lady Wootton says: 'that two separate propositions are inherent in Dr Glueck's position – first, that questions of responsibility can be by-passed; and, second, that criminality is itself a disease. Dr Glueck himself connects these closely, in effect deriving the first from the second. Nevertheless they are in fact distinct, and it is . . . possible to hold one without necessarily being committed to the other.'[37]

Certainly this is true. You could consistently believe the first for quite different reasons, or for no reason at all; while to believe the second surely commits you to saying that the question of responsibility is (not so much bypassed as) answered in the negative sense. But anyone who, like Lady Wootton, does want to maintain the first without presupposing the second, will have to be careful. It will not do for instance to take it for granted that to remove or to inhibit the inclination to delinquency will be 'for the good of all concerned', including the delinquent himself. For that will only be universally true upon a providential assumption which it would be very hard indeed to justify without appealing to the second, Platonic, proposition.

*

4   The more immediately astonishing thing about the statements at the beginning of the chapter on 'Mental Disorder and Criminal Responsibility' is the conclusion that the collapse of all attempts to develop a suitably objective distinction between mental health and mental disease must clear the way for assertions that all behaviour of some particular disfavoured sort is in fact a symptom of mental disorder. But, as has been hinted already, we should also be more profoundly astonished that Lady Wootton is prepared to suggest that such an attempt must be unsuccessful, notwithstanding that extraordinarily little direct attention has been paid to the crucial physical paradigm. Certainly she more than most others does notice its importance from time to time. But what, while she is considering and rejecting a series of suggested definitions of 'mental health' or 'mental disease', she significantly does not do is to ask herself how mental health or mental disease, so defined, would relate, or fail to relate, to ordinary health or regular disease.

Let us therefore at very long last raise the neglected fundamental questions, 'What is health?' and 'What is disease?' The Compact Edition of *The Oxford English Dictionary* suggests that Plato was right to pick out the idea of function as central. Health, it tells us, is 'Soundness of body; that condition in which its functions are duly and efficiently discharged'. Disease in the relevant sense is, correspondingly 'A condition of the body, or of some part or organ of the body, in which its functions are disturbed or deranged; a morbid physical condition; a departure from the state of health especially when caused by a structural change.'

A first objection is that this is in two respects too broad. It would include both those malfunctionings due to some congenital defect and those caused by wounds. But although doctors might hesitate to pass a man who is in consequence of some genetic defect blind as without qualification fit, his blindness could scarcely be rated as a disease. Similarly a person whose digestive processes have been deranged by bullet wounds in the stomach will be very seriously ill. He will not be diseased. The Royal Commission on the Law relating to Mental Illness and Mental Deficiency was taking account of the first of these two distinctions when it recommended the use of 'mental disorder' as the generic expression, with 'mental illness' and 'mental deficiency' as species labels.[38] The Commission found no corresponding merit in any mental analogue of the distinction between wounds and diseases.

A second objection is that these definitions fail to allow for the possibility that the malfunctioning may be delayed. For a condition may be said to be diseased in as much as either it is now resulting in, or if not suitably treated it will later result in, malfunctioning. (Here death is of course the limiting case of malfunctioning.) This possibility of delayed action is very practical. It is what gives point to programmes for regular physical check-ups on apparently fit and well people. To us its theoretical interest lies in the opening it makes for expert knowledge, not merely of the causes and cures of diseases, but also of whether a given condition is or is not diseased. Yet so long as disease is defined in terms of malfunctioning, and malfunctioning is something which it is in principle possible for the layman himself to recognise, the possibility of some delay in its actual manifestation makes no change in the nature of the expertise involved.

What would present new problems would be if the effects in the delayed action cases were of some radically different kind, and such that the patient himself could only recognise the threatened malfunctioning as really being such after some special course of self-transforming training. It is one thing – and very disturbing – for my doctor to tell me that, although I now both feel perfectly well and can do all the things which I can normally do, I am nevertheless the victim of a condition which will if untreated become both painful and incapacitating. It is quite another thing – and to the unregenerate natural man wholly undisturbing – to be told by some Platonic para-medical adviser that my present state, and that into which this will develop if I do not forthwith submit myself to his ministrations, are both such as I would, if only I were a quite different and much better person, utterly deplore. For in that second case I remain, such is my actual present so scandalous condition, complacently content.

The third objection is more fundamental. Although the idea of function is surely in some way central, Plato and the dictionary are both wrong in attending to actuality rather than potentiality. The tongue of a Trappist is not diseased merely because during a penitential fast it is employed neither in tasting nor talking. My rose bushes are not diseased simply because they are not taking in water which is not there. It will be time to begin asking questions about disease if when the Trappist eventually tries to exercise his tongue he finds that he cannot, and if when the bushes are inundated by a cloudburst still no water enters the system.

A fourth and still more important point comes out when those two examples are compared further. In so far as both show that what matters here is potentiality rather than actuality, they are the same. But in other respects they are crucially different. Suppose that water is supplied to my rose bushes, and that none is then absorbed. That will constitute a sufficient reason for inferring that there must be something organically wrong, although what is organically wrong will not necessarily be a disease. Contrast with this the case of the fasting Trappist. He is a person and not a plant. So the fact that he does not eat when food is provided is no more sufficient to show that there is something organically wrong than is the fact that he refrains from making passes at the pretty girls. In his case, but not in that of the plants, there is room for questions about what he can do if he wants and what he could do if he tried. Indeed it is essential to the description of this particular example that there actually is a gap between what he is doing and what he could be doing if he chose. For anyone who suggests that a dumb eunuch is fitted for a Trappist vocation is altogether failing to grasp what monasticism is about.

The fourth point, which applies to people and not to plants, is different from the third, which applies to both equally. The fundamental facts which give purchase to such questions about people are universally familiar and practically inescapable. Yet it seems to be difficult to describe these facts in a theoretically neutral way. The unfortunate consequence of failure is that the resulting theoretically loaded and thus legitimately controversial descriptions provoke those who cannot accept the overload to attempt to ignore or to minimise the facts themselves.

The facts which I therefore want at this stage merely to indicate and not to theorise about, are: that in the happy bloom of youth and health our bodies are partly, although still only partly, subject to our wills; and that there is a fundamental difference between for instance the claim that I moved my arm and the claim that my arm moved (although I did not move it).[39] Let us, in order to save words later, distinguish movements of the former sort as movings, while reserving the word 'motions' for movements of the second kind. And let us also, again for future reference, notice the dangerous possibilities of that favourite word 'behaviour'; which bridges – and which may therefore blur – this basic distinction between voluntary movings and mere motions. For these possibilities may be even more important than the fact that to employ this word as it is employed by behavioural scientists is to assimilate into a single category both what people say and what they do – two things which it is for many purposes necessary to be ready to contrast.

Now it is just not on to attempt to deny the subsistence of a difference: between on the one hand the case of – say – my liver, which however hard I try I cannot move at all except by shifting my whole torso; and on the other hand my little fingers, which I can wiggle around whenever and however the fancy takes me. But if in referring to such familiar differences I characterise the equally familiar possibilities of control as manifestations of the freedom of the will, then this affirmation may not be similarly uncontroversial. For, whether rightly or not, the word 'freewill' and the expression 'the freedom of the will' are often so construed as to imply some measure of indeterminism and radical unpredictability. Even if human beings and their affairs do happen in fact to be as believers in the freedom of the will in this philosophically libertarian sense believe that they are, that this is so is certainly not as immediately obvious and undeniable as the facts which I am trying to indicate.

Once these fundamental truths have been brought into the centre of attention we are ready to recognise a fifth point about the notion of (physical) disease in its primary employment. This primary application is surely to people and their organs, rather than to the brutes and theirs, much less to plants and theirs. But to say of disease in a person that it is 'A condition of the body, or of some part or organ of the body, in which its functions are disturbed or deranged' is to challenge the question whether these functions do or do not include besides mere motions some movings or abstentions from movings.

The response to this gets us to the heart of the matter. For the concept of capability, of what we can or cannot do if we try, is central to the notion of (physical) health – at least in its primary application to human beings. For a man to be fit is not for him to do, but only to be able to do, whatever it is which he is fit to do. Certainly, to be fit to do what a sick or otherwise unfit man cannot do, does in fact always require the actual or potential proper functioning of organs which never are subject to the will. Nevertheless the criterion of the fit man's fitness is: not the propriety of these actual or hypothetical motions; but rather his capacities for not necessarily proper movings and not movings. So, if a definition of 'disease' in terms of the disturbance or derangement of functions is to be retained, we shall have to take it that the function of whatever is normally subject to our wills precisely is to be in this normal way thus subject.

To illustrate this fifth point, consider malingering. The malingerer is the man who 'reports sick' when he believes that he is not. He pretends to be suffering from some disease, or to be otherwise unfit, in order to be excused from duties which he does not want to fulfil. His pretences, and the response of the authorities if they are persuaded that the malingerer genuinely is 'sick', are intelligible only in so far as what he is pretending to would involve some relevant incapacity. His supposed disease, that is to say, or other disorder, must be such as, whether immediately or later, to render the patient either incapable of doing at all, or at least incapable of doing so well, something which otherwise he could have been required to do, or could have been required to do better. No authority concerned to prevent the avoidance of the duties which it imposes can afford to allow that disease excuses, except in so far as the irregularities involved are relevantly incapacitating.

The sixth point about the dictionary definition is that in referring to disturbances or derangements of functions it is appealing to some sort of norm determining how things ideally ought to be. In thus picking out a normative element in the meanings of the words 'health' and 'disease' this definition is obviously right. But whereas it is easy to notice that this element is present, and to appreciate the consequence that medicine must be an essentially impure science, it is harder to explicate the nature and the content of the norms involved. One first sure thing is that disease is not, any more than is delinquency, something 'that is abnormal, by its infrequency of occurrence'.[40] For a disease, just like some forms of delinquency in some milieux, could be endemic and universal. As recently as the last century there used in fact to be even in Europe areas in which the entire population suffered from malaria. I am told too (by both Hungarians and Rumanians) that in the old, unregenerate, pre-conquest days Hungarian chauvinists would advise travellers: 'Where everybody steals, that's Rumania.'

Another sure thing, and one much more worth remarking, is that at least as regards disease the norms involved seem to be comfortably undisputatious. Where there is agreement about the clinical facts we do not expect doctors, even from very different cultural backgrounds and of quite opposite ideological persuasions, to disagree more than very occasionally as to whether a patient is or is not physically diseased. This comparative undisputatiousness in practice is a good reason for hesitating over the suggestion that these particular norms are to a significant extent culturally conditioned.

Such suggestions have been made in the seemingly somewhat sketchy literature. Thus Dr Lester King, in an essay on 'What is Disease?', gives the answer: 'Disease is the aggregate of those conditions which, judged by the prevailing culture, are deemed painful or disabling, and which at the same time deviate from either the statistical norm or from some idealized status.'[41]

But what actually is painful, and what actually is in some way disabling, does not depend on what the prevailing or any other culture may happen to believe. Where therefore there are differences on these counts someone has to be wrong on a point of fact. What does provide room for cross-cultural value conflicts is: not the question of what is a pain and what is a disability; but the secondary issue of which pains and which disabilities to be disturbed about, and which to take as tolerably normal. This scope is widened by the fact that the capacity to do one thing can often be bought only at the price of an incapacity to do something else. That massive build for instance which gave you your chance to be anchorman in the tug-of-war team must make it impossible for you to go to the bottom as a world-class caver.

To support his contention that the application of the concept of disease is culturally conditioned King refers to the artificial deformation of the daughters' feet in aristocratic families in traditional China. The example is inept, yet for that very reason it can be instructive. It would not surely be correct to describe the condition of the girl's feet – whether before or after the binding treatment – as diseased. Certainly that treatment made them unfit for either labour in the fields or table-tennis contests. Unfitness however can result from congenital defect or from mutilation as well as from disease. We have, without prejudice to any disputes about the ideals involved, to insist that this is not an instance of causing or curing disease. It is rather a matter of artificial deformation – or reformation. Certainly there can be, and indeed have been, cross-cultural conflicts about the practice of foot-binding; just as there have been, and indeed still are, about the categorically similar cases of male and female circumcision. But these disagreements are not, I submit, about whether the untreated are or are not as such diseased. They are about whether such treatments are proper, and whether their results constitute mutilations.

To all this the notion of disease becomes relevant only in so far as it may be argued that if such treatments promote health then they cannot be illicit, and their results cannot properly be abused as mutilations or deformations. This may be a plausible contention as regards male circumcision. But supporters of female circumcision and foot-binding were – or are – much more likely to refer not to general health but to adaptation for a particular social role. Here we certainly do find dramatic cases in which fitness for one way of life must be unfitness for another: for what fits a woman well for her prescribed role in traditional Kikuyu society necessarily unfits her to serve as an emancipated playmate for Mr Hefner's young men; while what fits a child to become an instrument of 'conspicuous waste' inevitably unsuits the adult for the heavier tasks required to realise the thoughts of Chairman Mao.

These dramatic cases illustrate how fitness for one role may preclude fitness for another. They are not however cases of health as opposed to disease. There seems to be no parallel example in which what doctors of one culture rate as a physical

disease is by their fellow doctors of some opposed ideology
accounted perfectly healthy. Indeed it is this comparative
undisputatiousness of the norms of physical disease which constitutes one, but only one, main reason why so many moralists
have been eager in one way or another to incorporate delinquency into the same category. For how very convenient it
would be if only conflicts over whether or not someone is at
fault could, like questions as to whether his physical condition
is diseased, safely be left to expert adjudication. If only too
those who have been at fault could always be handed over to
medical or quasi-medical experts in the secure knowledge that
their treatment would be for their own as well as for the public
good. 'We know', Boethius consolingly assures us, 'that in the
case of the soul health means goodness and sickness means
wickedness. And thus the protector of the good and scourge
of the wicked is none other than God, the soul's guide and
physician. He looks out from the watch-tower of Providence,
sees what suits each person, and applies to him whatever He
knows is suitable.'[42]

This undisputatiousness of the norms of disease, in so far as
they are indeed undisputatious, depends upon certain fundamental facts about organisms. It is typical of organisms that
they should be composed of non-redundant organs. It is this
familiar and perhaps somehow necessary characteristic which
enables both biologists and the Common Law to work on the
presumption that any organ does have a function even when
it is not at present known what that function is.[43] It is also a
fact that given sufficient data biologists generally find little
difficulty in agreeing on what the function or functions of any
particular organ are, and whether these functions are in fact
being discharged efficiently; and in harmony with the dis-
charging by other organs in the organism of their functions.
But there is and can be no similarly convenient consensus about
whatever in the human organism is subject to the will; except
of course in so far as, as has been suggested, the function here is
taken to be precisely and only that of being thus for better or for
worse subject to the will.

★

5   Further points about the concept of physical disease can
best be brought out by commenting on another suggested

definition. In an enumeration 'Of Circumstances influencing Sensibility' in *An Introduction to the Principles of Morals and Legislation* Jeremy Bentham wrote: 'Health is the absence of disease, and consequently of all those kinds of pain which are among the symptoms of disease. A man may be said to be in a state of health when he is not conscious of any uneasy sensations, the primary seat of which can be anywhere in his body.' (VI, 7)

It is characteristic of Bentham, but wrong, to make 'uneasy sensations' the heart of the matter. For someone can be easily unaware that he has a disease. This possibility was dramatically actualised in a recent British case, much quoted in the press overseas. A man picked up the victim of a traffic accident, left lying by the wayside, and drove him to hospital. There the doctors spotted that the Good Samaritan himself was all unwittingly subject to a disease which would, had it not been treated forthwith, have been fatal within hours. I do not know whether this particular disease would finally have caused 'uneasy sensations'. But it certainly is possible for even a fatal disease to be totally or almost totally painless. Happily this seems to have been the case with David Hume's terminal illness, the 'wasting disease of the bowels'. The same surely applies even more decisively in many of the cases in which someone is so fortunate as to die quite unexpectedly 'peacefully, in his sleep'.

By contrast it is also perfectly possible for some physical condition involving neither wounding nor hereditary defect to give rise to very 'uneasy sensations' indeed, without its thereby qualifying as a disease. The most obvious illustrations here are pregnancy and the actual process of childbirth. A woman can feel very ill during pregnancy, and may be more or less incapacitated by her condition. Nor in this event will things be made easier for her by the fact that these misfortunes are among those, like seasickness, to which other people who do not suffer similarly are apt to be unsympathetic. Yet none of this apparently is sufficient to warrant the diagnosis 'disease' when the condition itself and the culminating performance are both so indisputably instances of biologically normal functioning.

The truth, as was with something less than an unshakeable conviction suggested in the previous Section 4, seems to be that the core notion, in so far as there is a core notion, is that of malfunctioning. But since, as is most commonly insisted in discussions of the theologian's Problem of Evil, [44] the biological function of pain is to compel attention to some threatened or actual malfunctioning in or damage to the organism, it is usual for both wounds and diseases to be at some if not in all stages painful. However the system is of course not perfectly complete and effective. Just as there are some dangerous substances which we find attractively sweet-smelling, so there are some diseased conditions which are not signalled by any 'uneasy sensations'.

Even if we do not ourselves share Bentham's commitment to develop a comprehensive ethical and psychological Utilitarian theory, we may still be led astray by two pairs of more particular pulls. First Bentham's account of disease does in an appealingly simple way meet what earlier seemed to be two of the essential requirements. For if disease necessarily and not merely normally involved uneasy bodily sensations, then this would surely be sufficient reason to insist that it must always be presumptively and in itself bad for the sufferer. Suppose too – a little generously – that the reference to 'the primary seat' being 'anywhere in his body' is construed as excluding sensations produced directly and artificially by chastisement or other rough treatment, whether inflicted by others or by the patient himself. Then presumably the patient is now, even if earlier he could have avoided getting into this condition, a victim of the disease, which he cannot escape immediately and at will.

But this first pair of requirements is satisfied equally by our own insistence upon malfunctionings rather than painful sensations. Take the second first. Either the malfunctioning is confined to organs not normally subject directly to the will, and/ or it causes, or partly or wholly consists in, incapacities. This sufficiently guarantees that the patient who has actually got the disease cannot get rid of it immediately and at will; and hence that he must be to that extent, and in this respect, a victim. The rather awkward temporal qualifications are needed to provide for the fact that many patients could at some earlier stage have avoided getting into their present condition. For instance: both syphilis and gonorrhoea are by the exercise of a little timely prudence nowadays very largely avoidable; albeit often only at the price of using a sometimes unacceptable old-fashioned oral prophylactic – saying 'No', and meaning it. But such earlier avoidability is no more a reason for saying that the patients could now change their condition at once and at will, than their admitted present need of medical help is a reason for saying that they never had a chance of not getting themselves into this state.

The first requirement is that disease must be presumptively and in itself bad for the sufferer. This too can be satisfied by an account in terms primarily of malfunctioning. For in so far as the malfunctionings either cause, or partly or wholly consist in, incapacities; then they must surely be rated as, presumptively and in themselves, bad for the people concerned. Yet, as before, the various qualifications are essential. My disease must be presumptively and in itself bad for me; and it can be, notwithstanding that the fact that I am thus incapacitated may be a blessing for others. The illness which has the torture specialist of the political police lying helpless in his bed is presumptively and in itself bad for him; but it is certainly a fine thing for his intended subjects, and probably good absolutely. Again your tuberculosis must still be allowed to be presumptively and in itself bad for you; even though it is entirely to the fact that you have this disease that you owe your exemption from military conscription, and all which that may involve. It must be: since clearly it would be better still for you if you could both retain that exemption and recover your health; and since, equally clearly, your qualified satisfaction with your diseased condition can be made intelligible to the mean sensual man only by reference to particular present circumstances.

*

6   Of the second pair of pulls, which might mislead someone to accept Bentham's erroneous account of the nature of disease, the first is that that account carries the consequences that everyone must be his own best expert on whether he is himself diseased. The second is that, if Bentham is right, it is the seemingly negative notion of disease, and not the apparently positive concept of health, which – in J. L. Austin's memorably inelegant phrase – is the one 'to wear the trousers; commonly enough the "negative" (looking) word marks the (positive) abnormality, while the "positive" word . . . merely serves to rule out the suggestion of that abnormality'.[45]

Such attractions are not of course attractions for everybody;

far from it. Plato, certainly, would have found the first consequence repellent; while the second is necessarily rejected by
all who accept the ambitious definition presupposed in the
constitution of the World Health Organisation: 'Health is a
state of complete physical, mental and social well-being, and
not merely the absence of disease or infirmity. . . .' However to
appreciate what the attractions or, as the case may be, repul-
sions are is to see what matters here, and why.

So consider first the demand of John Stuart Mill, presented in
the 'Introductory' section of his essay *On Liberty*: 'Each is the
proper guardian of his own health, whether bodily, *or* mental
and spiritual.' Although a normative conclusion cannot be de-
duced from strictly non-normative premises, it would nevertheless have been convenient for all those who, like Mill, want to
defend politically libertarian norms if only it were the case that
each man is his own best expert to recognise whether or not he
does in fact have a disease – 'whether bodily, *or* mental and
spiritual'. That the italics at the start of that final clause are
Mills's, and that he chooses to employ the word 'guardian', may
well suggest to us that he himself had in mind exactly those
characteristically Platonic notions reviewed in the last three
sections of the previous part.

For the second attraction consider again the suggestion made
in Dr Walter Barton's grumbling Appendix to Marie Jahoda's
Current Concepts of Positive Mental Health: 'Conceptually, it is
difficult to see how a national program to reduce mental illness
and increase mental health can be operated on any other base
line than a straight one. In this continuum, illness is the point
of departure and health is the goal.'[46] Curiously, as was pointed
out when some of this passage was quoted previously, in Section
1 of the present Part, Barton himself says that his contention is
conceptual. Nevertheless, as he actually puts it, it is not. His
emphasis is upon what happens to be in present circumstances
practical and sensible: 'If we had solved, or even partially
solved, the problems of preventing or treating major and minor
mental illness, we could then justifiably concern ourselves with
the issue of superlative mental health, or the degrees of goodness in good mental health. Unfortunately, we still have far to
go in reducing illness.'[47]

Barton's proposal that we should for the foreseeable future,
if not perhaps for ever, concentrate on urgent cases of actual

illness, rather than on formulating and promoting some ideal
of positive mental health, is authentically Hippocratic. It constitutes an excellent reason for wanting to make out that the
negative idea of disease has some sort of conceptual priority
over the positive notion of health. To extend the methodological perspectives compare here Sir Karl Popper's antithesis
between the approaches of what he labels the piecemeal social
engineer and the Utopian.

Popper explains that for the Utopian the first rational step
is to formulate his positive ideal: 'Only when this ultimate aim
is determined, in rough outlines at least, only when we are in
possession of something like a blueprint . . . only then can we
begin to consider the best ways and means of its realization, and
to draw up a plan for practical action.' By contrast 'The piecemeal engineer will . . . adopt the method of searching for, and
fighting against, the greatest and most urgent evils of society,
rather than searching for, and fighting for, its greatest good.
This difference is far from being merely verbal. . . . It is the
difference between a reasonable method of improving the lot
of man, and a method which, if really tried, may easily lead to
an intolerable increase in human suffering. It is the difference
between a method which can be applied at any moment, and a
method whose advocacy may easily become a means of con-
tinually postponing action until a later date, when conditions
are more favourable.' It is in the second note to this chapter
that Popper, after insisting that there is 'no symmetry between
suffering and happiness, or between pain and pleasure',
advocates a negative as opposed to the traditional positive
utilitarianism: 'Instead of the greatest happiness of the greatest
number, one should more modestly demand the least amount
of suffering for anybody; and, further, that unavoidable
suffering should be distributed as equally as possible.'[48]

Just as it would be convenient for the political libertarian,
although this is not necessary to his essentially normative
position, if it were to have been conceptually guaranteed that
each man must be the best expert on whether he himself has a
disease or not; so it would be convenient – even perhaps just too
convenient – for the negative utilitarian, notwithstanding that
his stance also is essentially prescriptive, if he could point to the
concept of disease as being somehow logically prior to the
concept of health. Positive notions of health must be seen by

the negative utilitarian as threatening a diversion of energies from the most urgent task of relieving undisputed evils. They also constitute an at least equally serious threat to the concerns of the political libertarian.

Since everyone's health is presumptively and in itself good for him, anyone who promotes the health of someone else must be presumed to be his benefactor; and so any opposition to the treatment which the experts prescribe as necessary in their patients' own interests can only be the outcome surely of inexpert ignorance. The wider the scope of the concept of health, the wider the scope for such not necessarily welcome beneficence.[49] If psychological health is admitted as well as physical, then that area must be extended correspondingly. If we further proceed to construe health in general, and psychological health in particular, as positive ideals not definable in terms solely of the absence of the corresponding sorts of diseases, then 'mentally healthy' is almost bound to become a commendatory characterisation of some favoured life-style;[50] and then the more or less forcible imposition of that life-style, being now a matter simply of health, cannot but be seen as for everyone's own good.

There is of course no general objection to forming positive ideals or to recommending favoured life-styles. The objection is to doing such in themselves perfectly proper things in covert and illicit ways. To introduce any notion of mental health here is to pretend to endow your own chosen values with the independent and final authority of objective science. More subtly, it must be to discount as merely symptomatic utterance whatever might be said in favour of alternative recommendations. For to claim that my opponent is as such mentally sick is to arrogate to my personal preferences a scientific validity; and a validity which then happily relieves me of the sometimes too demanding task of rebutting his arguments.[51]

This first objection or, rather, these first two objections are not peculiar to the political libertarian. What characteristically concerns him is the possibility of appealing to such loaded notions of positive health in order to seem to justify the willy-nilly imposition of whatever ideals and life-styles may happen to be thus surreptitiously recommended. But he will of course be equally suspicious, and for the same reason, of all conceptions of mental health as essentially conformist – as necessarily requiring 'adjustment' to whatever may happen to be the ideas and powers that be. For in so far as both include the idea of health, both allow the possibility of insisting that any 'adjustment' required must be for the patient's own good.

In the review discussed in Section 1 of the present Part, Marie Jahoda accentuated the positive. And in the even more authoritative study noticed in Section 2 the authors began their consideration of 'The Nature of Mental Health' by making explicit 'two assumptions . . . that there can be different degrees of mental health; and that mental health is associated with principles dependent upon the prevailing religion or ideology of the community concerned. Therefore any attempt to define mental health involves consideration of the religious and ideological setting.'[52]

The dangers of such notions from a libertarian standpoint, which are therefore their authoritarian attractions, can be made more obvious by comparing the partly parallel development of positive concepts of freedom. Freedom, like health, is, by common consent, a good thing. It is therefore powerfully tempting to argue that so worthy an object cannot be merely negative. We are then told that true, positive, freedom is: not an absence of restrictions, which enables the free man to do or not to do what he himself wishes; but instead the fulfilment of some particular ideal, which is not necessarily – and is most likely not in fact – presently accepted by the actual all too human beings whom it is proposed to endow with this blessing. If so, too bad; they have to be forced to do or to accept what, because it is in their interests, they must really want. They must, in the most notorious words of Rousseau's *Social Contract*, 'be forced to be free'. (I, viii)[53]

So much then for the reasons why we may like, or dislike, the second pair of implications of Bentham's account of the nature of disease. Reasons were given earlier for rejecting that account as incorrect. It remains to ask now how far our own rival account provides for these implications.

Certainly it does not permit the first inference: 'that everyone must be his own best expert on whether or not he is himself diseased'. But any analysis which did carry this implication would certainly be wrong. For, as was urged as the second objection to the *Oxford English Dictionary* definition, it is perfectly possible for the doctors to know that the patient is ill when he himself believes that he is not; a possibility strikingly actualised in that case of the new English Samaritan, cited at page 43 above. However, as was suggested when this objection was first put in the preceding Section 4, there is no need for the libertarian to be especially disturbed by this possibility; provided only that the expected future development of the present painless but diseased condition is such as the patient can now, and without benefit of any special course of self-transforming training, recognise to be presumptively and in itself bad for him.

The threat, which as always is to others a promise, is that the diagnosis of disease, but especially of psychological disease, may be taken to license the experts to initiate transformations which their patients themselves regard now as for the worse. It was indeed precisely for such unwelcome exercises, in reshaping men in ways which perhaps regrettably they do not themselves recognise to be for their own good, that Plato's Guardians were by their para-medical knowledge supposedly qualified. But the way to neutralise this threat, or to frustrate this promise, is not, mistakenly, to insist that present illness must have present pain. It is rather to refuse to permit the application of the notion of psychological disease to cases which are not cases of disease at all. Above all it is to insist that 'mental health' and 'mental disease' must be defined not in terms of actual behaviour but in terms primarily of capacities and incapacities.

The second inference permitted if Bentham is right is that 'the seemingly negative notion of disease, and not the apparently positive concept of health . . . is the one "to wear the trousers"'. Happily there is no call for us to try to decide here how we are supposed to determine which is truly the positive and which the negative of a pair of terms each of which is definable as the negation of the other.[54] Nor do we need to worry even if it is suggested that health requires, besides the absence of disease, some sort of felt or seen glow. For in neither case will the negative utilitarian have much difficulty in making his essential point about priorities. The political libertarian too should again be well content with the insistence that the simple facts, that someone harbours unacceptable tastes, or that he expresses unpopular preferences, or even that he chooses to act in disfavoured ways, are neither separately nor together sufficient to show that he is in any way diseased. Full room has been left, as the political libertarian will insist that it must be, and as indeed it must be, for nonconforming protest: 'Do not adjust your mind; there is a fault in reality.'[55]

*

7   What is curious is that, by his taking the heart of the matter to be 'uneasy sensations' rather than actual incapacities, the legal reformer Bentham makes it harder to appreciate why a plea of disease can often be accepted as a completely sufficient excuse for failing to act in some required way. For pains surely could be relevant only indirectly and to the extent that they were either intolerably distracting or sheerly incapacitating; whereas if you were at the time in question relevantly incapable, then this is so immediately decisive that there is nothing more to be said. It is in this latter understanding of mental disease as characteristically if not essentially incapacitating that lawyers have been prepared to admit psychiatric evidence about the accused. Thus the famous McNaghten Rules, formulated in 1843 nine years after Bentham's death, insist that a man must be held accountable for his actions unless he was 'labouring under such a defect of reason, from disease of the mind, as not to know the nature and quality of the act he was doing, or, if he did know it, that he did not know he was doing what was wrong'.[56]

Since their first formulation these rules have been subject to increasing criticism on the grounds that they attend only to defects of reason – to incapacities, that is to say, to argue soundly and to understand what is what. In this of course they follow an ancient tradition. Some of its most quoted rulings will bear quoting again. One of the earliest comes from Bracton, who was a priest and head of the then highest English court, the Aula Regis. In 1265 he wrote in his *De Legibus*: 'The madman does not understand what he does, and lacks mind and reason, and is not far removed from the brutes.' In 1535 Fitzherbert, a judge of common pleas, provided a handy test of mental deficiency: 'An idiot is such a person as cannot count or number twenty pence, nor tell who was his father or mother, nor how old he is.' And in 1671 Sir Matthew Hale, a famous judge and author of authoritative legal treatises, insisted: 'Such persons as have their lucid intervals (which ordinarily happen between the full and change of the moon) . . . have usually at least a competent use of reason, and crimes committed by them in these intervals are of the same nature, and subject to the same punishment, as if they had no such deficiency. . . .'[57]

Certainly among lawyers the main objection to this traditional concentration upon intellectual incapacities has been, not to the insistence upon the question of capacity or incapacity, but to the exclusiveness of the concern with the intellectual. Thus in 1886 Judge Somerville in Alabama declared that 'there must be two constituent elements of legal responsibility in the commission of every crime, and no rule can be just and reasonable which fails to recognize either of them: (1) capacity of intellectual discrimination; and (2) freedom of the will'. Having earlier, with a fine sense of occasion, insisted that the Common Law is not 'like the law of the Medes and Persians, which could not be changed', and that 'its power of adaptation to new scientific discoveries, and the requirements of an ever-advancing civilization . . . must not be unduly obstructed by the doctrine of stare decisis', Judge Somerville proceeded to conclude that, if it is true as a matter of fact that mental disease can so affect the mind 'as to subvert the freedom of the will, and thereby destroy the power of the victim to choose between right and wrong, although he perceive it'; then the patient of such a disease must surely be, no matter how clear that perception, innocent victim rather than criminal agent.[58]

Substantially the same conclusion was reached rather earlier in England by Sir James Fitzjames Stephen. He proposed three rules to replace the McNaghten two, offering these confidently as an account of what the law ought to be, and only slightly less confidently as an analysis of what really it was already: 'No act is a crime if the person who does it is at the time when it is done prevented (either by defective mental power or) by any disease affecting his mind: (a) from knowing the nature and quality of his act; or, (b) from knowing that the act is wrong; (or, (c) from controlling his own conduct, unless the absence of the power of control had been produced by his own default).'[59] More than half a century later, in 1953, Stephen's third rule was endorsed as a proposal by the Royal Commission on Capital Punishment, but without the final exception clause. They recommended a change in the law to require that 'the jury must be satisfied that, at the time of committing the act, the accused as a result of disease of the mind or mental defect either (a) did not know the nature and quality of the act; or (b) did not know it was wrong; or (c) was incapable of preventing himself from committing it'.[60] This recommendation – which in Britain, incidentally, seems to have been submerged in the politicking about the outright abolition of the death penalty for murder – is in effect identical with that included in the Model Penal Code of the American Law Institute: 'A person is not responsible for criminal conduct if at the time of such conduct, as a result of mental disease or defect, he lacks substantial capacity either to appreciate the criminality of his conduct or to conform his conduct to the requirements of the law.'[61]

The same understanding of disease is again presupposed by two enormously influential American decisions. Mental, like physical disease, is then taken to be in itself or in its effects incapacitating, and whether someone is or is not the victim of any sort of disease is construed as a straight matter of fact. Thus in the case of *State* v. *Jones* (1871) the Supreme Judicial Court of New Hampshire maintained that 'Whether the defendant had a mental disease . . . seems as much a question of fact as whether he had a bodily disease; and whether the killing of his wife was the product of that disease was also as clearly a matter of fact as whether thirst and a quickened pulse are the product of a fever.' The legal implications are obvious: 'No argument is needed to show that to hold that a man may be punished for what is the offspring of disease would be to hold that a man may be punished for disease. Any rule which makes that possible cannot be law.'[62] Judge Bazelon, when he formulated in 1954 what has since been christened the Durham Rule, gave the alternative: 'simply, that an accused is not criminally responsible if his unlawful act was the product of mental disease or mental defect.'[63]

*

8   I have quoted extensively in the previous Section 7 from legal sources in order to bring out that it is precisely – and surely only – in terms of the sort of understanding being developed in the whole of the present Part II that questions of

disease, and particularly of mental disease, could be relevant to decisions of criminal responsibility. If 'mental disease' were definable, or in so far as it is allowed to become definable, simply and solely in terms of disfavoured behaviour as such; then the appeal to mental disease, so construed, would be, or must become, impotent either to explain or to excuse that disfavoured behaviour. Suppose for instance that for you 'kleptomaniac' is just a scientistic synonym for 'sticky-fingered': then necessarily, for you, to say that he is a kleptomaniac no more explains his characteristic thievery than to say that chloroform possesses anaesthetic virtue explains why it can put people to sleep; and, equally necessarily, the same utterance, from you, can no more serve to excuse that thievery than could its less pretentious equivalent of saying that he is of a thieving disposition. Again suppose that the presence of mental disease is, or suppose that it is allowed to become, not a matter of, albeit elusive, objective fact, but some sort of function of the ideological commitments and the social position of the observer. Then to say that he is mentally sick is, or would be, to say something at least partially on all fours with saying that he is – or more likely is not – one of our party, our religion, our class or whatever. It is precisely against the recognition of such irrelevant differences that Justice is supposed to be blind-folded!

If however we take mental disease, as we surely should, to be something which of its very nature tends to inhibit capacities, then it at once becomes obviously relevant to ask whether the accused suffered from some 'mental disease or mental defect' which rendered him incapable of understanding, or incapable of at will doing or abstaining from, whatever it was that the law required of him. And of course with appropriate alterations, the same applies in other, extrajudicial, contexts. It applies, that is, in all contexts of accepting or disclaiming personal responsibility, whether or not this accepting or disclaiming happens to involve inculpation or exculpation.

The second requirement which I have been stressing, that the diseased condition should be such as to be regarded by the patient as in itself and by his standards bad, is in the judicial context rather less directly relevant. First it is generally, for purposes of legal exculpation, sufficient to show either that your client did not know what he was doing, or that it was behaviour which he could not have helped anyway. Yet the case will certainly be strengthened if it can be shown that he would positively have preferred that what happened should not have happened, and that he is now eager that all possible steps be taken to prevent any recurrence. Supposing that this is indeed so, then he presumably must regard the condition apt to produce such regrettable and regretted behaviour as 'in itself and by his standards bad'.

Since in such contexts of judicial exculpation this suggested second requirement is thus less directly and not essentially relevant we can perhaps, at least sometimes, afford to neglect it. But when we are confronted directly with the problem of deciding what conditions can, and what cannot, properly be rated as mental diseases, then it certainly is essential, although not consequently sufficient, to attend to both requirements. However, since there may reasonably be doubt whether what I have formulated as a second requirement really is an element in the meaning of the expression 'mental disease' – as opposed to a peripheral condition which may normally be presumed to be satisfied as a matter of contingent fact – it becomes especially worth emphasising that the crux here is in any case not purely or even primarily conceptual. For suppose it is conceded that my 'second requirement' is in truth not a necessary condition of the correct application of the term 'disease' or the expression 'mental disease'. It still remains true that there is a world of difference, and a world of difference which must not be over-looked or concealed: between on the one hand the usual doctor/patient relationship, in which the doctor is trying to change a condition which the patient wants changed; and on the other hand another relationship in which, while the doctor is as before working for change, the complaints come not from the patient but from other people.

This important question of who is complaining first arose for us in the case of 'The Nut', described in Section 3 of Part I. Compulsory treatment, or confinement, were not immediate issues there. But it was being suggested – for absolutely no good reason given – that it was the uncomplaining husband rather than the very understandably complaining wife who was the victim of the disorder; and consequently that any treatment provided would be in the first instance in his interests and for his good. The same question is equally pertinent in far more serious

cases, where compulsory treatment and confinement may be
live issues. Dr E. Bittner of the Langley Porter Neuropsychiatric
Institute of San Francisco was therefore right to press it in the
discussion of a recent presentation by Dr R. G. McGrath. Dr
McGrath was speaking for the psychiatric staff of Broadmoor.
Dr Bittner with great tact objected:

> The patients in your charge are, as you put it, in need of 'the
> strictest control'. I appreciate that the talking about patients'
> needs as the governing consideration in treatment expresses
> the noblest aspects of psychiatry, but this is not completely
> realistic. Whatever these needs are, and I do not wish to dis-
> pute your appraisal of them, they are embedded in society's
> need to have the patients in such institutions as Broadmoor.
> . . . People are sent to institutions for the criminally insane
> . . . not only because they are sick but also because they
> are criminals and dangerous. In ordinary medical or psychi-
> atric practice the risk of incomplete recovery or recurrence is
> borne by the patient alone. In the treatment of the mentally
> abnormal offender the burden of the risk is distributed in
> the community.[64]

The same question will become even more to the point, and
may well need to be pressed less tactfully, where the justification
for confinement or for compulsory treatment is not so obvious,
or not obvious at all. Most of Dr McGrath's wards, if released
as they were when they were first confined, would presumably
constitute a clear and present threat of violence against
others.[65] It is reasonable enough to argue that such proven public
menaces should be confined in a special institution, and there
subjected to compulsory treatment; especially when, because
they have actually committed violent offences already, the
effective alternative is incarceration for a more definite term in
prison.[66] Yet even here one should be careful: not only not to
overlook that such imprisoned patients may not actually want
the treatment which will be provided by the public psychiatrist;
but also not to assume too easily that what undoubtedly is in
the general interest must necessarily and always be in the
interests of and for the good of each individual subject.[67]

Later in the same Symposium, to which both Dr McGrath
and Dr Bittner contributed, another psychiatrist, Dr A.
Schapiro of Harperbury Hospital at St Albans, argued: 'When
we talk about the compulsory detention of mentally abnormal

offenders, we are not talking about criminals but about very ill people. One may detain and treat, if necessary surgically, an unconscious patient in hospital, assuming that he would have consented to treatment if he had been conscious. The great innovation in England and Wales came in 1959 with the Mental Health Act, when psychiatrists were allowed to treat people incapable of consent without judicial permission. . . . The duty of society towards a handicapped member is to treat him as a minor or as someone who cannot take responsibility for his own treatment.'[68]

It is of course entirely right in all discussion of mental disease to search for the physical analogies. But the one to which Dr Schapiro appeals cannot give him the mileage he wants. Comparatively few physical diseases are so catastrophically disabling as to render the patient unable to give or to withhold a valid consent to treatment; and even Dr Schapiro's fellow psychiatrists, especially those engaged in more private practice, would surely take a lot of persuading to accept that the situation is in this respect altogether different with mental diseases. I suggest too, although I obviously am in no position to prove, that direct examination even of Dr Schapiro's own patients in Harperbury Hospital – an examination, that is, which did not appeal to the supposed consequences of their being mentally diseased – would not justify any general claim that they are one and all chronically incapable of anything deserving the name of considered consent or refusal. They may all be – I am sure that they are – thoroughly misguided and often very dangerous in what they want or do not want. But that is not at all the same thing as being, like a man unconscious, simply unable to consent or to refuse. If they really were all in that way and to that extent helpless there would be no security problem in his or any similar institution.

The great danger here – and for all such public psychiatrists it is a true occupational hazard – is to insist from the beginning that your dealings with your wards are exactly those of a (private) doctor with his (physical) patients. Being conscious of your own purely and perfectly Hippocratic intentions, you then infer that – since to cure (physical) patients of their diseases is (normally) to act in their interests, and to respond to their needs, and to do what they themselves want you to do for them – all this must apply equally to you and your situation.

Certainly the argument is as sound as the intentions are honourable; and none the less so because – like Dr Schapiro – you
may have confused yourself further by mistaking it that what
holds of only a minority even of seriously ill physical patients
holds of all. But a sound argument guarantees its conclusions
only where its premises are in fact true.

The present argument takes it for granted that the patients
in question are indeed suffering from mental diseases, and that
in an interpretation in which mental diseases must be in the
crucial respects like physical diseases. This is the interpretation
which I have throughout the present Part been trying to develop
and to defend; and I have been correspondingly concerned that,
if we are to infer from statements that someone is mentally
diseased the conclusions which do indeed follow, then we must
demand that the original statements are appropriately warranted. Notwithstanding that it is constantly done, it will not
do to begin by assuming or even asserting that since we are
dealing with serious mental disease this or that must be the
case, and then to overlook the instances where in fact it is not;
and to fail to see that, if these consequences do not obtain, then
that they do not is a ground for concluding that – whatever may
or may not be wrong with that subject – 'mentally diseased' just
cannot be the correct description of his condition. There is and
can be no substitute for looking directly at the facts; and asking,
of each separate candidate type, whether or not the analogy
with the physical actually is adequate to justify the description
'mental disease'.

★

9   It is a task which might fill many books, and perhaps
never be completed. But what is needed here and now is to
establish some paradigms: first some sorts of case to which,
upon the basis of that crucial analogy with the physical, the
application of the description 'mentally diseased' is clearly
warranted; and then others in which, by contrast, notwithstanding that such a diagnosis has in fact been rendered by
some qualified psychiatrists, it is equally clearly not justified.
Certainly there must remain many further actual or possible
cases which are far more marginal, and where the correct
verdict would necessarily be less obvious. But a sure way of
producing not clarification but confusion is to start by attend-

ing to peripheral or derivative employments of the term or expression under examination without first getting a strong grip on what is typical and fundamental.

So let us start where Freud himself started:

> The obsessional neurosis and hysteria are the two forms of neurotic disease upon the study of which psychoanalysis was first built up, and in the treatment of which also our therapy celebrates its triumphs. . . . The obsessional neurosis takes this form: the patient's mind is occupied with thoughts that do not really interest him, he feels impulses which seem alien to him, and he is impelled to perform actions which not only afford him no pleasure but from which he is powerless to desist. . . . Against his will he has to worry and speculate as if it were a matter of life and death to him. The impulses . . . mostly . . . consist of something terrifying, such as temptations to commit serious crimes, so that the patient not only repudiates them as alien, but . . . guards himself by prohibitions, precautions and restrictions against the possibility of carrying them out. . . . What he does commit are very harmless, certainly trivial acts – what are termed the obsessive actions – which are mostly repetitions and ceremonial elaborations of ordinary everyday performances, making these common necessary actions . . . into highly laborious tasks of almost insuperable difficulty . . . he is perfectly aware of his condition, he shares your opinions about his obsessional symptoms. . . . Only he simply cannot help himself; the actions performed in an obsessional condition are supported by a kind of energy which probably has no counterpart in normal mental life.[70]

For our theoretical purposes it is perhaps a pity that Freud has to say of the kind of patient who has these 'impulses . . . to commit serious crimes' that: 'As a matter of fact he never, literally not even once, carries these impulses into effect. . . .' Yet there can be no doubt but that obsessional neurosis, as here described, does deserve to be called a disease. Freud keeps insisting that the patient 'is powerless to resist', that 'he simply cannot help himself'. So, once granted that this is indeed true, it follows that the obsessive and compulsive actions must be – in our terminology of Section 4 of the present Part – not movings but motions; which brings with it the rather awkward consequence that such obsessive and compulsive actions cannot in the strictest sense be actions at all. Since the malfunctioning here has at any rate no known organic foundations, it can be taken simply to consist in the fact that what would be subject to the will in a normal person, in the patient is not so subject. Its cure must, correspondingly, simply consist in the correction of that malfunctioning. It must, that is to say, be helping the patient to regain those powers of which he had by his illness been deprived.

That a cure should be in the eyes of the patient himself and by his standards in itself good is in this paradigm case provided for twice over. It is in effect stipulated in Freud's specification: '. . . he is perfectly aware of his condition, he shares your opinions about his obsessional symptoms . . .', and so on. But it is also, and more interestingly, guaranteed by the very nature, as Freud now proceeds to describe this, of a psychoanalytic cure. He starts from 'a fundamentally new fact, by means of which much else becomes explicable'. This new fact is that: 'Symptoms are not produced by conscious processes; as soon as the unconscious processes involved are made conscious the symptom must vanish.'[71] Now Freud surely cannot be claiming that the therapy which makes the unconscious conscious thereby renders patients who previously could not help performing some obsessional ritual now equally unable to repeat that performance – in the excessively unlikely event of their wishing so to do. So to warrant the conclusion that 'as soon as the unconscious processes involved are made conscious the symptom must vanish', it has to be assumed that the patient himself wants to be shot of his symptomatic obsessional performances (motions); and hence that he will not – once the success of the therapy has given him the choice of going through the ritual or not – repeat the same old routine as a series of true actions (movings).[72]

It is essential, if we are to appreciate what was involved in Freud's introduction of his idea of the unconscious mind, to take the measure of this supposed 'fundamentally new fact'. For – as I have argued at length elsewhere – the heart of the matter is, that, 'if you are prepared so to extend such notions as motive, intention, purpose, wish, and desire, that it becomes proper to speak of motives which are not known to, and the behaviour expressing which is not under the immediate control of, the person who harbours them; then you can interpret (and even guide) far more of human behaviour in terms of concepts of this sort than any sophisticated adult had previously realised.[73]

The immediate relevance of this for us lies in the second of the two extensions: 'that it becomes proper to speak of motives which are not known to, and the behaviour expressing which is not under the immediate control of, the person who harbours them.' This second innovation was of the two the more radical, and yet it is also the one more often overlooked. Even Dr Thomas Szasz, in his splendid crusading onslaught on *The Myth of Mental Illness*, seems not to appreciate how crucial it is.

As the title of his book suggests Szasz undertakes to show: not just, as I would agree to be both true and important, that the concept of mental illness has been dangerously abused and absurdly overextended; but rather, what is surely false and extravagant, that it has no proper application at all – that there simply is, and perhaps can be, no such thing as a mental disease. In his Introduction he says: 'I submit that the traditional definition of psychiatry . . . places it alongside such things as alchemy and astrology, and commits it to the category of pseudo-science. Psychiatry is said to be a medical specialty concerned with the study and treatment of mental illness. Similarly, astrology was the study of the influence of planetary movements and positions on human behaviour and destiny.'[74]

Szasz begins with a chapter on 'Charcot's Contribution to the Problem of Hysteria'. For he rightly takes this contribution to have constituted the historical turning point, and hysteria to be one paradigm of what mental disease has been supposed to be. Szasz quotes from Freud's memoir, 'Charcot':

> First of all Charcot's work restored dignity to the subject; gradually the sneering attitude, which the hysteric could reckon on meeting when she told her story, was given up, she was no longer a malingerer, since Charcot had thrown the whole weight of his authority on the side of the reality and objectivity of hysterical phenomena. Charcot had repeated on a small scale the act of liberation commemorated in the picture of Pinel which adorned the lecture hall of the Salpêtrière. Now that the blind fear of being fooled by the poor patient which had stood in the way of a serious study of the neurosis was overcome, the question arose which mode of procedure would most speedily lead to the solution of the problem.[75]

It certainly is curious, as Szasz insists, that Freud speaks here only of Charcot's authority: and that Freud does not here commit himself by actually saying that these particular patients were not in fact malingerers. Instead his whole emphasis – and this was a noteworthy sign of the shape of some things to come – was upon two fortunate consequences of Charcot's influential reclassification: first that it restored human dignity to its subjects; and second that it encouraged study where previously this had been inhibited. Szasz takes Freud's reserve to be an indication that those whom Charcot thus asserted to be suffering from the mental disease of hysteria were in fact, after all and with whatever justification, malingerers. Szasz therefore proceeds to assemble further and more direct evidence to confirm suspicions of Charcot, 'the Caesar of the Salpêtriere'.[76]

Suppose we allow that Charcot himself was often, or even always, deceived by malingerers. It still remains an extraordinarily bold thesis to maintain that there never have been any genuine cases of hysteria or obsessional neurosis, satisfying the descriptions provided by Freud and by so many others; and hence that there cannot have been any authentic cures of these conditions, either by Freudian psychotherapy, or by any other treatment. It is therefore surely significant that Szasz in his turn does not himself actually say precisely this, in so many words. Instead he goes on in a second chapter to discuss 'The Logic of Classification and the Problem of Malingering'.

It is here, I suggest, that he fails adequately to come to terms with the second of the two aspects of Freud's notion of unconscious motivation. Szasz says: 'With Freud and psychoanalysis hysteria comes to be viewed as unconscious malingering. . . . This new version of malingering . . . differed from the previous notion of counterfeit illness (of the body) by virtue of the new dichotomy "conscious-unconscious".'[77] This is to bungle the playing of Freud's hand. For on the interpretation just now provided Freud ought to say of the patient suffering from an hysterical paralysis or given to obsessional and compulsive performances: not only that he, or she, is not aware of the motives engaged; but also that he, or she, is unable to move the paralysed member or, as the case may be, unable to stop the compulsive performances. But any 'malingering' which is in this dual sense unconscious is not malingering at all. For it is necessarily authentically incapacitating. There is therefore no reason for denying that here is a case of disease.

*

10   Yet it is mental rather than physical. In as much as our concern is with mental disease in its relations to delinquency, attention has to be concentrated upon what is required to warrant the application of the second term in the expression 'mental disease'. But it should at least be noticed that the scope of this expression is properly in part determined by whatever is from time to time seen as constituting the essence of the mental. Plato, as we saw in Section 8 of Part I, construed his ψυχή [psyche] as a word for a sort of incorporeal substance; taking all the behaviour which distinguishes men as rational agents as the manifesting work of these themselves unobservable entities – which are, he thought, what men ultimately and essentially are. This provided, at any rate in theory, 'a satisfyingly clear-cut and decisive principle for separating the spheres of physical and psychological medicine'. However although much of the talk of the activities and interactions of the Unconscious and the Preconscious and the Conscious, of the Ego and the Id and the Superego, does encourage interpretation along such Platonic lines, it is at least doubtful whether any contemporary psychiatrists – with the possible exceptions of 'some Roman Catholics and Catholicising Jungians – really intend their theoretical notions to be read in so substantial a way.[78]

Traditionally, as came out clearly from the review of legal tests in Section 7 of this Part, the crux has been taken to be knowledge and understanding. Thus Philippe Pinel, who did so much to ensure that the insane should be treated as mentally diseased, saw their afflictions as consisting in disorder in this area: 'The storms of the revolution stirred up corresponding tempests in the passions of men, and overwhelmed not a few in a total ruin of their distinguished birthright of reason'; and a memorable example of such a cataclysm is provided by the unfortunate patient who believed that he had been first guillotined, and then afterwards reconstituted – if that is the right word – with someone else's head.[79] But, as we also saw in the same Section 7, this rationalist conception was already being widened long before Freud.

In Freud's own paradigm cases of mental disease, as he describes them, there specifically is not any untowardness of belief: the patient 'is perfectly aware of his condition, he shared your opinions about his obsessional symptoms. . . .' The introduction of Freud's conception of the unconscious carried with it the adoption of a new and much more comprehensive criterion of the mental: a man's mind became, it might be said, the entire field of application to him of all such intentional notions as motive, purpose, wish and desire; while, at the same time, the objects of all these concepts are allowed to be, if they are not conscious, unconscious.[80] The description 'mental disease' can consequently now cover: not only afflictions which reduce the rational capacities of the patient; but also any condition in which acquired incapacities are the expressions of unconscious motives. By either criterion of the mental, narrow or broad, all mental disease presumably must be at the same time disease of the central nervous system; although those who presume this are not required to take it that the converse is true also. Certainly Freud, who was an alumnus of the Vienna Medical School and a disciple of Brücke, remained always faithful to the conviction that all psychological phenomena have some determining physiological basis.

Now if, like any other scientifically minded person, you want to say this;[81] and if you also want to allow, as rightly or wrongly almost everyone does, that there really are cases of a kind for which Freud's description of obsessional neurosis provides a paradigm; then you will have to allow that there are, for practical purposes, two very different sorts of disease of the central nervous system: 'Mental illnesses can be broadly subdivided into those which are clearly associated with an identifiable cerebral abnormality, and those which are not.'[82]

This is the distinction here between on the one hand the organic, and on the other, the functional. The temptation is to believe that as indices of incapacity the organic afflictions possess an ultimate epistemological superiority over the functional. Thus, to cite an old but famous example, in the trial of Hadfield for the treason of attempting to murder George III, the task of Lord Erskine for the defence was greatly eased by the fact that he could display to the court visible brain damage: 'His client had obvious and disfiguring wounds in the head. . . . One . . . had penetrated the skull, so that Erskine was able to invite the jury to inspect the membrane of the brain itself. An officer of his former regiment testified that before Hadfield had been wounded he had been an excellent soldier, but afterwards had been incoherent, with "manifest symptoms of derangement". The regimental surgeon recalled how he had been compelled to have Hadfield tied to a bed for a fortnight.'[83]

Even waiving the further sympathetic consideration that Hadfield's injuries had been suffered in the service of his country, and against the French, this evidence was all that Erskine could have asked. The jury too, confronted by such gross brain injuries, were quite right to be very ready to accept evidence that these injuries had produced equally gross mental derangement. What justified this readiness was the other knowledge which they already had of ways in which such injuries and deformities give rise to incapacities. But this knowledge can provide no basis for denying the practical possibility that people may become afflicted with incapacities which have no presently detectable physiological basis. Much more interesting are two less familiar points. First it is certainly not apriori necessary that every difference in the capacities of two objects must be grounded on, and a manifestation of, some structural difference between those objects. If this actually is the case – as of course every good materialist must believe – that it is the case is a matter of contingent fact. Second the ideas of function and capacity are here epistemologically prior and not secondary to the notions of injury and disease. For a condition could not be identified as diseased except by reference primarily to its tendency to frustrate functions and to inhibit capacities.

The relevance of these abstract and metaphysical considerations to practical questions about delinquency and mental disease is this. Especially among those made impatient by attempts to excuse any and every crime as an expression of mental disease, there may be an inclination to urge that the only genuine and potentially exculpatory mental diseases are those which are satisfyingly organic, and not merely functional. This is in effect the position into which in *The Myth of Mental Illness* Szasz imprudently manoeuvres himself. The imprudence of it comes out most clearly when we entertain the permanent possibility of discoveries requiring the transfer of some condition previously rated as only functional into the other, the organic, category. If ever, or whenever, this possibility is realised those who have denied the genuineness of the incapacities which had previously been presented as only functional will have humbly to admit that these were after all authentic. But the temptation to adopt such an indiscreet position will be further reduced once it is also realised, as has just been argued, that there is no apriori necessity that capacities and incapacities should always be bottomed upon structural differences, and that these ideas here are in any case epistemologically prior to that of disease.

In this perspective it becomes clear too that – granted always one crucial proviso – there can be no objection in principle, though there may be many of substance, to admitting into the category of functional mental disorders pyromania, kleptomania, homicidal mania and indeed as many other kinds of mania as the combined resources of our Classical knowledge and our imagination permit us to compass. The crucial proviso is that the disease, if it is to be a disease, must be defined: not in terms of the mere inclination towards the disfavoured behaviour; but in terms of an inability to inhibit that inclination.

At the beginning of Section 8 of this Part, I maintained that: if 'for you "kleptomaniac" is just a scientistic synonym for "sticky-fingered": then necessarily, for you, to say that he is a kleptomaniac no more explains his characteristic thievery than to say that chloroform possesses anaesthetic virtue explains why it can put people to sleep; and, equally necessarily, the same utterance, from you, can no more serve to excuse that thievery than could its less pretentious equivalent of saying that he is of a thieving disposition.' This is, I still think, all absolutely right. But the implications become quite different if 'kleptomania' is defined, not in terms of thieving as such, but of compulsive thieving; or, at any rate, they do so as long as 'compulsive' is construed as meaning (more or less) uncontrollable.[84] For, on that interpretation, that he is a kleptomaniac is (more or less) an excuse for his stealing; in his condition he would have found it (unusually hard or) impossible not to have stolen. It is also just worth pointing out that, on either interpretation, to say that he is a kleptomaniac can help to explain why he committed one particular theft. What it cannot explain, since it is a restatement of it, is his general disposition to steal, or to steal compulsively, as the case may be.

So if kleptomania, or pyromania, or whatever, is construed

as compulsive thievery, or compulsive incendiarism, or compulsive whatever, then such a condition, if it does in fact occur, may with good reason be categorised as mentally diseased; and the compulsiveness which is necessary to justify this classification should also be sufficient to excuse the behaviour. But it is a different thing again if these terms are to be construed, as they sometimes are, as referring to the absence of any normal, and hence immediately and generally intelligible, motivation. He had no reason to steal, it may be said, and such a silly and useless lot of objects too: he could afford to buy all the paperclips and light bulbs and protractors which he needed; and anyway his apartment was awash with ones which he had already stolen from other places. She had no reason to burn those places down: she did not even know the owners, much less have grudges against them; and the buildings were not even insured, so she could not have hoped to collect on that.

Such conduct cannot but be puzzling. It certainly seems irrational. For the agent had no motive – no reason – for so acting. Or – rather – the agent had no motive, no reason, with which we can immediately sympathise. Such conduct and its motives – conduct which, significantly but misleadingly, we are inclined to label 'motiveless' – could even be described, in a sense long on disapproval if short on literal content, as morbid. But it would be as wrong, and wrong for the same reasons, to define 'mental disease' in terms simply of deviant motivation as such as we have already argued that it must be wrong to define it in terms of deviant behaviour as such. Certainly deviance of motivation cannot by itself constitute an excuse for any conduct in which that motive is expressed. As Lady Wootton put it, in exactly the present context: 'It is by no means self-evident that the physician's yearning for valueless porcelain figures is inevitably stronger or more nearly irresistible than the poor man's hunger for a square meal or for a packet of cigarettes.'[85]

Furthermore not only will the definition of 'mental disease' in terms of motivational deviance make mental disease culturally relative in a way in which physical disease is surely not, but it may also introduce into some of the disease labels then proposed a curious factor of built-in obsolescence. For if for instance those old favourites 'kleptomania' and 'pyromania' are to be defined as in effect 'thievery and incendiarism for which there is no motive with which we can sympathise'; then that self-same sympathetic attention which we are required to give to the kleptomaniac and the pyromaniac as the patients of diseases must tend progressively to disqualify whatever we had initially been inclined to call kleptomania or pyromania. For we shall then argue – as anyway we could, and surely should, have argued before – that we all know perfectly well what it is to want something. Of course his wants strike most of the rest of us as very queer. But then no doubt there is some of what we want which would not appeal to him. So we can, and do, sympathise. The situation thus becomes like that in the story of the eighteenth-century landscape architect, who was labouring to impress a reluctant prospect: 'One quality I try to give to all my work is, unexpectedness.' 'Oh yes,' his interlocutor responded, 'and what is that called after your clients have got used to it?'

*

11   In Section 9 paradigms were provided of conditions which have been, and clearly should be, rated as mentally diseased. The paradigms of those which have been, but equally clearly should not be, so rated are all and typically conditions where mere deviance, whether of behaviour or of motivation, has been accepted as sufficient to warrant such classification. Traditionally the dimension of deviance which psychiatrists have been most inclined in this way to favour, or to disfavour, is the sexual. Thus in 1863 the then Director of the Edinburgh Royal Asylum listed satyriasis and nymphomania along with insanity of masturbation: the last was of course the supposed independently identifiable consequence of juvenile excess; whereas for the two former conditions the criteria appear to have been either the supercharged desires themselves, or the above Kinsey-par frequency of performance itself. (Although both these conditions could be described as, in a very literal sense, clinical, one may perhaps be permitted to wonder, parenthetically, how often any psychiatrist nowadays opens his consulting-room door to discover a voluntary patient himself complaining of any such complaint?)[86]

Twenty years later Kraepalin, whose *Textbook* was to become for several decades standard, included 'conträre Sexualempfindung' in his first *Compendium* as – along with idiocy, cretinism and feeble-mindedness – one of several 'States of psychological weakness'. In 1887 in the first edition of his *Short Textbook* the same conditions are listed as 'Developmental abnormalities'. Between the 693-page fourth edition of 1891 and the 815-page fifth edition of 1896, Kraepalin's work finally crossed the line which – even in Germany – separates a *Short Textbook* from a *Textbook*. In the resulting *Textbook* we find that 'Psychopathic conditions (degeneracy, insanity)' include the now familiar 'conträre Sexualempfindung', although at last glossed as '(psychic hermaphroditism, homosexuality)'. Much later, at the end of the Second World War, the United States Veterans' Administration in its Standard Classification, under the general heading 'Character and Behavior Disorders' and the subheading 'Pathological Personality', gives as items four, five and six respectively, 'Inadequate personality', 'Anti-social personality', and 'Sexual deviate'. Even later still, in 1952, the American Psychiatric Association keeps up the bad work by listing 'Sexual deviation' in its official *Diagnostic and Statistical Manual of Mental Disorder*: all such nonconformity is counted as a form of 'Sociopathic personality disturbance' – along with anti-social reaction, alcoholism and drug addiction.[87]

This will not do. For unless 'mental disorder' is to be construed here, perversely, as simply equivalent to 'nonconformity in tastes or behaviour', sexual deviation cannot be put down as a kind of mental deficiency or mental disease. There is surely, at least typically, no incapacity by which the deviant can be distinguished from the straight. Those homosexual sexual relations between consenting adults in private, which used in a less enlightened period of the English public law to be crimes, could not take place at all if the apparatus were not in working order; and even the exclusive homosexual is presumably as able, albeit as disinclined, to engage in heterosexual intercourse as the comparably exclusive heterosexual is able, yet not willing, to undertake any homosexual endeavour. Nor is there any reason to believe that the expression of their respective inclinations in what Hollywood advertisers used – before the four-letter revolution – to call 'acts of love' is any more, or any less, compulsive in the one case than in the other. The gift of continence would seem to be equally available to both; and equally unacceptable.[88]

Certainly, as a character trait, homosexuality is not under the immediate control of the subject. But then neither, for exactly the same reason, is heterosexuality. No doubt there are many homosexuals who would like to change their sexual tastes; although the number of those who are thus themselves complaining of their putative complaint must surely be enormously inflated by the addition of members of the very different class of those who are not so much girding at their homosexuality itself as wanting to remove the occasion of more intrinsically disagreeable, socially imposed disadvantages. But where the homosexual has no desire to alter his condition, as such, there would seem to be absolutely no scientific basis for putting him down as mentally diseased. Writing of 'the inverted' back in 1905, Freud made the crucial distinction: 'Some take the inversion as a matter of course, just as the normal person does regarding his libido, firmly demanding the same rights as the normal. Others, however, strive against the fact of their inversion and perceive it as a morbid compulsion.'[89]

Before deciding whether the condition of these others is, in a strict and meaty sense, morbid, we have to ask whether the resulting homosexual desires are peculiarly irresistible. If, and where, and in so far as, they really are; then perhaps the conditions of those, but only those, homosexuals who are indeed thus affected can be admitted as mentally diseased. The analogy will presumably be with alcoholics and hard drug addicts; although even such genuinely compulsive homosexuals will not, like the alcoholic or the hard drug addict, also be on a road to physical ruin.

But where even undesired homosexual desires are not peculiarly irresistible, then the subject's condition would seem to be strictly on all fours with that of many a Christian celibate longing to be rid of his wholly heterosexual cravings. The intellectual temptation here, a temptation to which Freud himself was not entirely immune, is to take it that biological structure is somehow normative; and hence to urge that homosexual sex must be, because unnatural, diseased.[90] Even if homosexual activities were always wrong, and even if this conclusion could be validly inferred from purely biological premises, that would still not be enough to show these disfavoured activities to be symptoms of a disease. For, as I have argued repeatedly, 'mental disease' cannot properly be defined in terms of either disfavoured behaviour or disfavoured inclinations as such; and without benefit of incapacity.

*

12   My second example is malingering. Since this is something which in Section 4 of the present Part I urged that genuine disease is essentially not, it may be suspected that I have fabricated a man of straw. But no: in fact it was discovered, not invented; and its special value to us is as a memorably bizarre specimen of what can – and does – result from letting talk of mental disease lose touch with the physical original. One source is an article, called simply 'Malingering', written by Dr K. R. Eissler on the basis, we are told, of his experiences as a psychiatrist with the United States Army during the Second World War: 'It can rightly be claimed that malingering is always the sign of a disease, often more severe than a neurotic disorder because it concerns an arrest of development at an early phase. It is a disease which to diagnose requires particularly keen diagnostic acumen. The diagnosis should never be made but by the psychiatrist. It is a great mistake to make a patient suffering from the disease liable to prosecution. . . .'[91]

Suppose that the first of these four statements were true, its truth would remove any foundation which there might otherwise have been for the second and the third. For wherever there really is an invariable sign of any disease; then there cannot be any difficulty in the diagnosis – other of course than whatever difficulty there may be in recognising that sign itself. Then again, in so far as this particular sort of sign genuinely is present, the presence of that new disease to which it supposedly points so infallibly could scarcely constitute a sufficient warrant for the fourth and final statement. For, in the words which concluded Sir James Fitzjames Stephen's account of the three rules proposed to replace the McNaghten two, 'an act may be a crime although the mind of the person who does it is affected by disease, if such disease does not in fact produce upon his mind one or other of the effects above mentioned in reference to that act.'[92] But, since the symptomatic malingering is by the hypothesis genuine, the disease cannot be preventing the agent: either '(a) from knowing the nature and quality of his act; or (b) from knowing that the act is wrong; or,

(c) from controlling his own conduct. . . .' It cannot therefore be producing 'one or other of the effects above mentioned'.

There remains the instructive question of what such a disease could consist in. Since it is apparently undetectable by anything save the most penetrating psychiatric analysis its severity cannot involve immediate suffering or present disablement: we need no specialist help simply to discover our aches or our aphasia. So it has to be a matter of what the future has in store. What needs to be, but is not, established is that the malingerer (not even but rather especially) if undetected, will come to a bad end. It is in this context irrelevant to the point of frivolity to appeal only to a hypothetical past with virtually indiscernible current consequences – 'an arrest of development at an early phase . . . which to diagnose requires particularly keen diagnostic acumen'.[93]

Yet Dr Eissler is no lonely and isolated eccentric, weaving moonbeams from some private lunacy. For one of the most distinguished psychiatrists in North America, Dr Karl Menninger, is prepared to maintain as the established view of his profession that malingering is itself a mental disorder:

> There is another type of personality deformity which is so ancient and classical, so commonly approved to be prevalent, and yet so rare, that we must list it out of sheer curiosity. It is the compulsive deception represented by the feigning of disease. Curiously enough the individual who does this, the malingerer, does not himself believe that he is ill, but tries to persuade others that he is, and *they* discover, they think, that he is *not* ill. But the sum of all this, in the opinion of myself and my perverse-minded colleagues, is precisely that he *is* ill, in spite of what others think. No healthy person, no healthy-*minded* person, would go to such extremes, and take such devious and painful routes, for minor gains that the invalid status brings to the malingerer.[94]

No one whose military career was made at a level less stratospheric than that traversed by Dr Menninger in the Second World War could, surely, bring themselves to believe that the rewards of successful malingering must always be, compared with the effort involved, minor. Yet that is not the most fundamental objection. For even if the straight majority who reported for duty found as much difficulty in empathising with the delinquents and the deviants as he and his 'perverse-minded colleagues' apparently do, that would still not justify their inclusion of malingering in the medical category of disease. However, were all malingering in fact compulsive, then this categorisation would be perfectly correct. Connoisseurs of the paradoxical will relish the thought that this would make mental disease impossible to sham: if you want to seem to have it then, necessarily, you must actually have it. For since, by the hypothesis, all malingering is compulsive, any performances which anyone intends – and even perhaps uninstructedly believes – to be pseudo-symptoms must nevertheless in fact be genuine compulsive actions; and to be afflicted by these is, paradigmatically, to be mentally diseased. However the incredible premise, from which this preposterous conclusion is derived, is itself supported only by appealing to that original disease classification which is itself here in dispute. Certainly if malingering really were (the expression of) a mental disease this would have to involve some compulsions or inhibitions somewhere. But to show that it in fact is we should need some, indeed much, direct and independent evidence. Instead we are offered only one more variation upon a by now familiar theme. In the background there is the constant general assumption that delinquency or even mere deviance either is, or ought to be regarded as, an expression of mental disorder. In the foreground we have a particular claim about a particular complaint, supported in effect by nothing more than the insistence that the delinquency or the deviance itself constitutes the criterion of the real presence of the postulated mental disease.

*

13   My third example is psychopathy. This has been defined as 'a mental disease which develops before or during puberty, caused by inherited predisposition, or by acquired personality deviation due to psychic or somatic factors or both, which, in turn, cause superego deficiency; it is characterised by stereotyped deviations in the moral, social, sexual and emotional components of the personality, without intellectual impairment, psychosis or neurosis, with lack of . . . insight or ability to profit from experiences, and is of lifelong duration in almost all cases.'[95] The Royal Medico-Psychological Association offered a very similar account in their evidence to the Royal

Commission on the Law Relating to Mental Illness and Mental Deficiency, which reported in 1957. Psychopaths, they said, are persons whose 'daily behaviour shows a want of social responsibility and of consideration for others, of prudence and foresight and of ability to act in their own best interests. Their persistent anti-social mode of conduct may include inefficiency and lack of interest in any form of occupation; pathological lying, swindling and slandering; alcoholism and drug addiction; sexual offences, and violent actions with little motivation and an entire absence of self-restraint, which may go as far as homicide. Punishment or the threat of punishment influences their behaviour only momentarily, and its more lasting effect is to intensify their vindictiveness and anti-social attitude.'[96] (By specifying not psychopathological but only 'pathological lying, swindling and slandering' the Association just, if only just, avoids the most glaring circularity.)

All this, as another expert witness admitted later, makes the term 'psychopath' as here expounded substantially equivalent to the expression 'moral defective', as introduced and defined in the Mental Deficiency Act of 1927; except that there is no firm claim that a psychopath must be intellectually incompetent.[97] So it is not surprising that the Mental Health Act of 1959, which followed the recommendations of this Royal Commission, provided that, for the purposes of the Act, ' "psychopathic disorder" means a persistent disorder or disability of mind (whether or not including subnormality of intelligence) which results in abnormally aggressive or seriously irresponsible conduct on the part of the patient. . . .' But the definition in the Act ended significantly, although in the face of the final clause of the first account just quoted perhaps also optimistically, 'and requires or is susceptible to medical treatment'.

If we ignore for the moment that last hope, what is remarkable about all three definitions is the lack of any good reason for according to the condition as specified the status of a disease. For, as I have been insisting all along, 'The core of illness is victimisation. . . .'[98] But my superego deficiency is not, like my toothache, bound to make me suffer. It is, immediately and in the first instance, other people who suffer from my unreliability and my unscrupulousness. So in so far as this deficiency is in any way at all my misfortune it must be indirectly and secondarily, less universally and reliably, and perhaps only in so far as the others have taken effective steps to protect themselves. Nor, as was similarly suggested in considering *Erewhon* back in Section 9 of Part I, are my dispositions to 'pathological lying, swindling and slandering' conditions which I can be presumed to wish to have relieved.

Consider for instance the description, from a presentation cited earlier, of the 'young agile, intelligent psychopath who has already killed while absconding from a Borstal Institution, is preoccupied with ideas of escaping, has seriously assaulted members of the nursing staff, and is cheerfully open in his preparedness to kill again in the course of escape'.[99] There is here absolutely no hint of any suffering or incompetence on the part of the 'patient'; and his own attitude towards the treatment to which he is compulsorily subject is surely made sufficiently manifest by his expressed willingness to kill anyone who stands in the way of his escape from Broadmoor.

As has been remarked by others previously, albeit with little apparent effect, psychopathy and the psychopathic personality thus seem to provide paradigm cases of the 'pious perjury' by which a supposedly excusing condition is more or less openly defined in terms of precisely that behaviour which it is then supposed to excuse. But the correct morals have not always been drawn. Lady Wootton for example, robust as ever, speaks of the psychopath as 'in fact, par excellence, without shame or qualification, the model' of this 'circular process'. Yet the moral which she draws is that 'the psychopath makes nonsense of every attempt to distinguish the sick from the healthy delinquent by the presence or absence of a psychiatric syndrome, or by symptoms of mental disorder which are independent of his objectionable behaviour.'[100]

This is an extraordinary conclusion to draw from these observations; and that this is the conclusion which she does draw is explicable only by reference to her own proposed ultimate conclusion. This ultimate conclusion is: that we are, and ought to be, moving towards 'abandoning the concept of responsibility'; that we are, that is, and ought to be, shifting the 'emphasis in the treatment of offenders away from considerations of guilt and towards choice of whatever course of action [appears] most likely to be effective as a cure in any particular case'.[101] Being an active and experienced magistrate, and no sort of psychological visionary, Lady Wootton proceeds almost at once herself to insist upon the likelihood that the claims of reform and deterrence, of cure and prevention, will be found in practice to conflict. If this is so, and it surely is: 'It is futile to uproot one blade of grass by methods which encourage the proliferation of others.'[102]

What is extraordinary about her immediate conclusion – and it is this which is our immediate concern – is that it neither follows nor even seems to follow from the observations. For where the term 'psychopath' is employed in the way indicated, there psychopathy quite clearly cannot be a disease. It is therefore: not the existence of such psychopaths which is making 'nonsence of every attempt to distinguish the sick from the healthy delinquent'; but rather the muddled persistence of some psychiatrists and others, who will go on rating both this and any and every other variety of disfavoured deviance as a mental disease. The true moral to be drawn here about psychopathy is that given in a statement quoted with approval by Lady Wootton herself a few pages earlier: 'It would seem . . . that until the category is further defined and shown to be characterised by specified abnormality of psychological functions, it will not be possible to consider those who fall within it to be unhealthy, however deviant their social behaviour.'[103]

Both words in the expression 'psychological functions' need to be stressed here: for unless the malfunctioning were, either in its origin or in its nature, psychological the disease could not be accounted mental; and unless to have the functions were to be construed as possessing capacities rather than being characterised by dispositions, there would be no reason to pick out the abnormality as a disease. To satisfy the necessary condition just laid down it would not be sufficient simply to meet the objection that ' "Psychopathy" is . . . a term like "lumbago", which purports to be a diagnosis but is in fact only a name for the symptoms.' To meet that objection it would be enough to find any way at all 'of identifying psychopaths independently of their behaviour' qua psychopaths. We should therefore, on that lesser task, be well away: either if we could point to studies suggesting 'that many psychopaths have abnormal electroencephalograph waves, showing a predominance of large slow waves, like those of young children';[104] or if we could discover some other behavioural characteristic, logically independent of all those involved in the definition of 'psychopath', which is as a matter of contingent fact shared by all and only those who are, in the sense specified, psychopaths.

But that would not necessarily get us very far towards establishing that psychopathy, so construed, is after all a disease. It is important to see exactly why. The temptation is to recall how for instance in 1822 Bayle showed that progressive paresis is a disease of the brain, or how in 1861 Paul Boca found lesions in the cortex correlating with certain forms of aphasia; and then to mistake it that the discovery of aberrant brain waves must therefore be sufficient to show that psychopathy is an authentic disease. But the cases are totally different. For there was no question but that progressive paresis and these kinds of aphasia were diseases; whereas what has to be shown here about psychopathy is, not that it has some physiological basis, but that it is a disease. No one doubts but that the aphasia patient, unlike the Trappist monk, is the victim of a speech disorder. But there are those who, whether rightly or wrongly, do doubt whether – or at any rate how completely – the scandalously anti-social conduct of the psychopath is truly to be attributed to his incapacity, as opposed to his disinclination, to behave better. In order to establish, therefore, the desired conclusion by reference to some physiological condition or phenomenon, it is necessary to show, not only that that condition or phenomenon is suitably correlated with psychopathy, but also that it is relevantly disabling.

For the present quite particular purpose it is not helpful to argue – or, more likely, simply to assume – that, absolutely generally, if any conduct has physiological sufficient conditions, then what was done could not have been something which could have been done, or not done, at will. This is certainly a seductive notion, which we shall have to examine in Part III. But it is far too powerful to introduce into a limited and regional conflict. For if it really is the truth, and if too the physiologists continue to make the sort of discoveries which they have been making, then the eventual implication seems to be: not, particularly, that the psychopathic behaviour of those previously identified as psychopaths in fact consists in – as it were – compulsive or reflex actions, and hence that psychopathy can after all be put down as a mental disease; but rather, generally,

that the whole notion of things being done or not done at will
– and hence all those other notions too which presuppose this
contrast – in fact lack any application at all. To show this, if it
could be shown, would not be to establish the existence of one
more species of mental disease, but instead to unleash a total
categorial catastrophe.

So long however as the term 'psychopath' continues to be
so used as to make psychopathy not really a mental disease,
we ought to recognise ' "psychopathic" and "wicked" as
belonging to two distinct sets of terms which are no more
mutually exclusive than terms dealing with physical beauty
and those dealing with physical health'.[105] Suppose psychopathy were a mental disease, we could not say that the (uncontrollable) behaviour resulting from it was either wicked or – at
least under the Durham Rule – criminal. But since it is not, we
may say, without contradiction and truly, that there is some behaviour which is both psychopathic, and wicked and criminal.

*

14   The conclusion of Section 13 in no way prejudices
the possibility, notwithstanding that psychopathy as presently
understood is not in fact a mental disease, that we may nevertheless decide to regard it as one, to treat it as if it were.
Indeed, for reasons indicated in Section 1 of Part I, precisely
this conclusion is presupposed by the very making of any such
suggestions, strictly interpreted.

One good reason why psychopaths convicted of serious
crimes should be compulsorily committed to mental hospitals
rather than to prisons is given by the last statement in the
quotation from the evidence of the Royal Medico-Psychological Association: 'Punishment or the threat of punishment
influences their behaviour only momentarily, and its more
lasting effect is to intensify their vindictiveness and anti-social
attitude.'

But although good this is not of course an indefeasibly good
reason. Even looking no further than those three initial quotations, we may object that the phenomenon described in the
first scarcely satisfies the final requirement of the third; since,
if psychopathy 'is of lifelong duration in almost all cases', we
cannot easily say that it now 'requires or is susceptible to

medical treatment'.[106] This objection however could be under-mined at any time by the advance of the art. Another, which we have just heard from Lady Wootton, and which is too often ignored by the prophets of psychiatry, is likely to be a more permanent obstacle: 'It is futile to uproot one blade of grass by methods which encourage the proliferation of others.'

If the psychopathic offender is to be committed to mental hospital rather than to prison, not because he is the victim of mental illness, but simply because he is incorrigibly recalci-trant, then this must surely have its effects upon all the rest of us actual and possible criminal offenders. Certainly it is impossible to determine apriori what all these effects will in fact be; and surely too our reactions will be considerably influenced by how protracted and how disagreeable the psychiatric treatment is (believed to be); compared with the traditionally penal alternative. But the theoretical crux, which is also of the most fundamental practical importance is, that the proper primary purpose of a penal system is: neither retribution on offenders; nor the reformation or cure of offenders; but rather the prevention of offences.

It is therefore wrong to focus on depressing rates of recidi-vism, and then from these alone to infer – in words which have become again a catch-phrase – 'that the whole system has failed'. Obviously it has failed either to reform or to deter those who, as the figures show, keep coming back for more. But any such figures are inherently incapable of showing either that the penal system has failed, or how well it is succeeding, in its most vital and fundamental task of maintaining by its silent presence the general framework of law and order. The system as a whole is in this respect like sea-power, in the description of Admiral Mahan: 'Those far distant storm-beaten ships, upon which the Grand Army never looked, stood between it and the dominion of the world.'

This most fundamental function of a penal organisation is frequently forgotten by the prophets of orthopsychiatry. Thus Dr Karl Menninger, whom we have met twice before, presses the general thesis that all crime should be treated as disease, and all criminals as patients: 'I would say that according to the prevalent understanding of the words crime is *not* a dis-ease. . . . It should be *treated*, and it could be; but mostly it isn't.'[107]

A few pages later he writes, with an emphasis reminiscent of a much-quoted dictum of F. H. Bradley: 'We have admitted that most criminal behaviour is not a disease . . . crime is still a wilful and avowed breaking of the rules, a flagrant disobedience, a flaunted infraction.' This shows that Dr Menninger's contention here is indeed what I have just said that it is; and that he is not recklessly embarking upon a universalisation of what he is elsewhere willing to urge, so unbelievably, about malingering. He even goes on to admit – albeit in a manner strongly suggesting that he is preparing to backslide – a crucial difference which many psychiatrists are remarkably reluctant to notice: 'Most recognised illnesses, however disagreeable to society, involve some conspicuous suffering or disability' for the subject. The propensity for committing crime does not *look* like suffering, nor does it cause any obvious disability'.[108] But in his conclusion Dr Menninger peers forward towards a rosier future: 'When the community begins to look upon the expression of aggressive violence as the symptom of an illness, or as indicative of illness, it will be because it believes doctors can do something to correct such a condition. At present some better informed individuals do believe and expect this. However angry or sorry for the offender, they want him "treated" in an effective way so that he will cease to be a danger to them.'[109]

It is certainly sad, even though it is perhaps also realistic, to think that, if 'the community' became persuaded that some particular sort of delinquent disposition could be straightened by whatever are from time to time to be accounted psychiatric means, then it would immediately infer that that disposition must be 'the symptom of . . . illness, or . . . indicative of illness'. It is sad, because this immediate inference would not be correct. Suppose we take the very strongest case, by construing 'psychiatric means' as being as exclusively physiological as anyone could wish. Now, unless the seductive but potentially catastrophic notion of Section 13 happens to be true, there seems to be no inconsistency in saying of some behavioural disposition: both that it could be inhibited by the agent himself, if he so wished; and that it could be corrected by some direct physiological manipulation, if only there actually was someone who knew enough physiology, and possessed sufficient manipulative skill. Since the inference is supposed to be immediate, no one can be entitled here to help themselves to 'the seductive notion' as a further premise; and so we may for the moment ignore that parenthetic proviso.

Significantly, when Dr Menninger turns from the unenlightened many of 'the community' to the few 'better informed individuals', the concern is entirely for the transformation, by whatever may be shown to be the most effective ways, of the actual offender: 'so that he will cease to be a danger to them'. This narrowness of view, which is altogether typical both of Dr Menninger himself and of many other psychiatrists discoursing on criminological themes, is no doubt in large part an expression of their professional training: doctors, or at least doctors within the Hippocratic tradition, are taught to concentrate upon individual patients; and to devote themselves to helping these patients as sick individuals.[110]

No doubt too it is another manifestation of that same training that when, as here, it is proposed that something which is not in fact disease should be treated as if it were, or when, as in some of the cases indicated in Section 8 of the present Part, this is perhaps actually happening, the doctors concerned should be so slow to appreciate how radically such ongoings must transform traditional concepts of the function of the doctor and of the doctor/patient relationship. For there most surely and obviously is a world of differences: between on the one hand acting as a patient's agent, in order to help him – as a professional man serves his client – to get rid of a disease, which he sees to be bad for him, and which he himself wants cured;[111] and on the other hand acting as the agent of some collective, in order – by employing knowledge which in general we do not in fact as yet possess – to change someone in directions in which he may not himself wish to be changed, and in which it is not necessarily, either by him believed to be in his interests, or even actually in his interests, to be thus changed.[112]

A different reason why the prophets of psychiatry so often find it hard to recognise the importance of deterring the non-offender is that they are reacting against their own excessively black picture of the old dispensation; and as usual the revolutionary new order is in important respects conditioned by and continuous with the old. Since, in the rather jaundiced view to which they are inclined, the whole object of the exercise

under the old regime used to be to ensure that criminals should
suffer the just retribution for their crimes; under the new
dispensation the whole object of the exercise will become a
forward-looking attempt to transform offenders – and maybe
others too – into good citizens who will never again commit
offences. Both the supposed old and the proposed new share
the same indifference to what should be the primary, preventa-
tive, function of the whole penal system.[113]

It is worth citing briefly two of many possible authorities
to show that such a blinkered concentration upon retribution
as the aim was by no means universal even in those dark ages
before we and enlightenment were born. The first is the great
Common Lawyer Sir Edward Coke, writing in the 1630s:
'The principal aim of punishment is, that others by his example
may fear to offend, ut poena ad paucos, metus ad omnes,
perveniat (in order that the penalty may touch a few, but the
fears thereof touch many).'[114] The second is F. H. Bradley,
examining 'The Vulgar Notion of Responsibility' in 1876.
No one has ever put more vehemently the basic moral point
that, while the right to punish is given always and only by the
committing of an offence, the nature and extent of that punishment may, and indeed should, be determined partly or wholly
by considerations quite other than those of proportionate
retribution:

> We pay the penalty because we owe it, and for no other
> reason; and if punishment is inflicted for any other reason
> whatever than because it is merited by wrong, it is a gross
> immorality, a crying injustice, an abominable crime, and
> not what it pretends to be. We may have regard for whatever
> considerations we please – our own convenience, the good of
> society, the benefit of the offender; we are fools, and worse,
> if we fail to do so. Having once the right to punish, we may
> modify the punishment according to the useful and the
> pleasant; but these are external to the matter and cannot
> give us the right to punish, and nothing can do that but
> criminal desert.[115]

★

15   Section 14 insisted that any proposal to treat crime
as an expression of mental disease, where in fact it is not, must
take account of two very different sorts of consideration. First

the prime proper function of a penal system is neither, particularly, to reform offenders nor to deter them from recidivism.
It is, generally, to prevent offences. Second the offenders who
are thus by the hypothesis not in fact mentally diseased have
not, presumably, themselves asked for psychiatric or any other
treatment. So there is no good reason to believe that such treatment must be in what they think are – or even what actually
are – their interests.

The penal system may be, it was there suggested, still
fulfilling its indispensible primary function even though – indeed perhaps especially when – it is rare for citizens to consider committing offences, only to be deterred by fear of
punishment. For the crucial questions of effectiveness here are
hypothetical. It is not: 'What does lead me to act or to abstain,
as things now are?'; but rather, 'What would I have been
doing had I not been raised within the protections and re-
straints of this system?'; and 'What should we all very soon find
ourselves suffering, and doing, if the penalty enforced framework of law and order were either to be dismantled or to
collapse?'[116]

To the second sort of consideration urged in the previous
Section 14 two points made much earlier are again relevant.
First, as was said first in Section 9 of Part I, it cannot be taken
for granted that what the psychiatrists will do to offenders will
always be less disagreeable to the offenders than whatever
might be the going, conventionally penal, alternative.

Second, as was indicated in Section 8 of the present Part,
although it sounds, and may even be, more enlightened to
provide treatments adjusted to each particular individual
rather than to inflict standard general penalties determined
largely or wholly by the nature of the offence; such progressive
proceedings have, from the point of view of both offenders and
possible offenders, one enormous disadvantage. This disadvantage is that, whereas the typical penal sentence is for some
limited term and probably reducible by good conduct, to be
instead detained at the psychiatrist's pleasure is to be imprisoned indefinitely.[117]

Two citations may perhaps be a salutary help in driving
these rather unfashionable points home. The first is from the
decision of Judge Richard S. Heller in the frightful and, I hope,
unparalleled case of *Dennison* v. *State* (1966). The New York

Court of Claims awarded $100,000 to Stephen Dennison, who had at the age of sixteen stolen $5 worth of sweets, and who had in consequence been forcibly detained in mental institutions for thirty–four years: '. . . the hospital records repeatedly described claimant's behaviour as paranoid, or in lay terms, that he had delusions of persecution. If a person is, in fact, being treated unjustly or unfairly, the fact that he perceives, resents and reacts to the inequity could hardly be regarded as competent and conclusive evidence of paranoia or paranoid tendencies. . . . In a sense, society labeled him as subhuman . . . insane, and then used the insanity as an excuse for holding him indefinitely.'[118]

This nightmare case does most memorably underline the point about the indeterminacy of such therapeutic sentences; and it can be suggestive in other ways too. Yet no doubt it was the botched work of some very bad psychiatrists. The second quotation comes from the Report, mentioned in Section 2 of the present Part, of the Scientific Committee of the World Federation for Mental Health: 'The term "brain-washing" has . . . been applied with unfortunate connotations to psycho-therapeutic practice by those who are hostile to it. We con-sider that the lesson of this needs to be taken to heart by all those who are responsible for securing psychiatric treat-ment of non-volitional patients. The use of compulsion or deceit will almost certainly appear, to those who are un-friendly to or frightened of the aims of psychotherapy, to be wicked.'[119]

It is one thing, and perhaps licit or even sometimes impera-tive, for a doctor to tell confident falsehoods to a patient who does not wish to hear discouraging truths. It is, whether wicked or not, quite another for Guardian psychiatrists to employ such 'noble falsehoods' when these are to be true lies told to help cure false diseases.[120] Brain-washing is a different thing again. There are some, and surely will be many more, possible treat-ments which it would not merely appear to be, but be wicked to inflict upon what the Committee so prissily describes as 'non-volitional patients'. Some of these may, like electro-convulsive therapy or the use of the drug aminazin, raise constitutional questions about 'cruel and unusual punish-ments'; at least in countries so fortunate as to possess old-fashioned Constitutions, enforcibly independent of the day-today wishes of the Party and the Government. The theoretical interest for us however lies elsewhere.

The expression 'psychiatric treatment' can cover an enormous variety of ongoings: from purely verbal transactions at one extreme, talk by a couch or even across a table; up to and including at the other extreme brain-surgery and dosing with drugs. The legitimate anxieties about brain-washing arise about treatments of the latter kind; especially if these are to be enforced upon people who, though not perhaps suffering from any genuine mental disease, must certainly be in this most important respect victimised. It will not do, as the Committee does, to discount all such anxieties as the inconsiderable verbalisings of those 'unfriendly to or frightened of the aims of psychotherapy'. By doing this they are making the same kind of mistake, and for fundamentally the same reasons, as those who held Stephen Dennison in various psychiatric prisons for four-and-thirty years. They are, that is to say, registering what is said: not as an argued objection, which has to be met; but merely as a symptomatic utterance, which constitutes here only an obstacle to be circumvented.

For suppose that it became possible simply to overpower someone, to strap him to the operating table, and – quite painlessly, employing whatever anaesthetics were medically suitable – to implant tastes to taste; to excise habits as indicated; to establish beliefs as required; and even to determine particular choices at will. Such a supposition may seem, in the present state of the art, to be far-fetched and purely speculative. Yet it involves only an extrapolation from what has long been familiar. Already in the nineteenth century William James could draw on many cases in which drastic personality changes had resulted from brain injuries. Twenty or more years ago reports were coming in of the effects of that notoriously hit or miss operation prefrontal leucotomy: of the woman for instance who was cured simultaneously, not only of her suicidal depressions, but also of her liking for classical music, and of her religious beliefs; which pre-operant illusions she now, to the din of pop, rejects as humbug.[121]

Still more interesting to us is a claim made on behalf of the neurologist Dr Harvey Cushing: 'The association centres discharge into certain incito-motor centres, which are among the best known regions of the cortex. . . . If we give them a mild electric shock, as was first done by Dr Harvey Cushing, with the consent of a patient, the subject moves his limbs, and does so with a full sense that he is voluntarily performing the action. This is quite different from the effect of stimulating the motor nerves in the spinal chord, or nearer still to the muscle. Then the patient merely feels his limb contract involuntarily.'[122]

Now to overpower someone, and to bring about a change in him by any such direct physiological manipulation, would be totally different from bringing about the same change: either by persuasion; or by coercion; or even by the very same physiological operations if performed at his own request. A similar difference will be found also, although not often quite so sharply marked, with many other less drastic psychiatric treatments. The crux is that such direct and unrequested physiological manipulation, however well-intentioned, however humane its methods, must be – as nowadays it is even by some of its most outspoken advocates seen to be – an outrage against the freedom and dignity of 'responsible and autonomous man'.[123] For it leaves its patient with no choice whatsoever as to how, or whether, he is to change or be changed. It treats him as a thing, to be shaped at the psychiatrist's will; not as a person, with the capability and the rights to make decisions for himself. Some words from C. S. Lewis's onslaught upon 'The Humanitarian Theory of Punishment' are to the point: 'To be "cured" against one's will, and cured of states which we may not regard as disease, is to be put on a level with those who have not yet reached the age of reason, or those who never will, to be classed with infants, imbeciles, and domestic animals. But to be punished, however severely, because we have deserved it, because we "ought to have known better", is to be treated as a human person. . . .'[124]

We need to get absolutely clear just how wide the gulf here is. Misleadingly we often say that we had no choice when what we mean is, not that we had literally no choice at all, but that we did indeed have a choice, but one in which all but one of the available options could be ruled out immediately as altogether unacceptable. Martin Luther for example was not confessing to a sudden paralysis when he thundered his magnificent protest to the Diet of Worms: 'Here I stand. I can not other. So help me God.'[125]

Much the same applies in the special case of acting, not of one's own freewill, but under compulsion. The man who acts under compulsion, unlike the man who has an irresistible psychological compulsion to act, acts. He does have alternatives. He may plead perhaps that he was compelled to open the safe because 'Pretty Boy' Floyd was fingering the trigger of his trusty Thompson; and fair enough. But of course he did have a choice. He could, and, had it been a matter not of the bank's money but of national security or of loyalty to comrades struggling against the Occupiers, he surely should have told Floyd very firmly and rudely what he could do with that machine-gun.

It is precisely and only because compulsion does in this way still leave the agent with his choice that it can be reasonable to require, as usually we do, that the seriousness of the threat which is to be acceptable as the excuse of compulsion must be proportionate to the gravity of the offence to be excused. Thus our elder daughter's unwonted rudeness to her teacher is abundantly excused by reference to the fact that a big and nasty boy forced her to do it by threatening to spill ink over her new dress. Yet a similar appeal on behalf of an adult would be dismissed as a bad joke in a trial for grand larceny; while the Nuremberg Tribunals did in fact rule that the certainty that disobedience to orders would have been fatal was not enough to expunge the guilt of helping to process people through the ovens of Maidenek and Auschwitz.

All such cases are entirely different from that of the man who is seized by main force; and then thrown, quite helpless, through the window. Unlike the other man who – perhaps under compulsion – jumps out of the window, the human projectile is not as such an agent at all. Since he does not act, he does not act either of his own freewill or under compulsion: he really does, quite literally, have no choice. The unwilling victim of direct physiological manipulation would be, in this respect, like the human projectile. But his case would be, in another way, far worse. The defenestrated man may after his fall be able to pick himself up and walk away none the worse, and none the better, for his experience; save perhaps for a few cuts and bruises, and a grudge against the assailant bully boys. But, in so far as the treatment has been successful, the other unwilling subject must be to a greater or lesser extent a changed

person. He may indeed be much improved; like another folk-
lore figure, some will recall irreverently, who had also been
exposed to radical surgery. Nevertheless the change in him will
not be a change which he wanted, or which he chose, or which
he made. Since even the fact that a change would be decisively
for the better is not a universally sufficient reason for effecting
it by coercion, it must be even less sufficient to warrant the
wholesale employment of this kind of irresistible personal
programming.[126]

★

16   Dr Harvey Cushing's demonstration demands separate
attention. For, although our reporter concluded his account
with the statement that 'The bearing of these facts on the
question of the Will is obvious', it is not equally obvious just
what those implications are. But what little can be said about
that within the tight limits of the present essay must wait till
Part III. Here the immediate corollary is again to insist that,
that some human condition could be altered by psychiatric
treatment, is not a sufficient reason for saying that that condition is mentally diseased. This emerges most clearly when we
concentrate on all those treatments, realised or possible, to
which, if imposed upon 'non-volitional patients', the term
'brain-washing' might fairly be applied. It then becomes easy
to remember the general truth that for you to be able, whether
with or without my assistance, to achieve some result is no
guarantee that I could not, if I so wished, make it entirely on
my own. Still less is it any guarantee that that result is either
one which I want or one which would be in my interests.

Though obvious to us now, these truths are often overlooked:
' "I call this condition an illness just because there is a medical
treatment for it, which experience has shown to be effective".'[127]
The same unsound principle may be one of the foundations
of the commitment law of the Commonwealth of Massachusetts; with or without its equally unsound running mate, the
principle that disfavoured behaviour as such can properly be
a criterion for mental disease. For in that jurisdiction, apparently, a man may be sent down for a stretch in a mental hospital
if the public psychiatrists testify that he 'is likely to conduct
himself in a manner which clearly violates the established laws,
ordinances, conventions, or morals of the community'.[128]

Since any promotion in Massachusetts of (what Roman Catholics distinguish as) artificial birth-control has long been, and at the time of writing remains, illegal, this illiberal and preposterous law opens the zany possibility that some recklessly conscientious body-doctor might, as a result of prescribing contraceptives, be confined in the custody of a group of his colleagues, the public mind-doctors; there to remain until such time as they shall succeed in straightening him to the line laid down in the Encyclicals *Casti Connubii* and *Humanae Vitae*. So far as I know this commitment law has never been applied to such a person. But I can cite two actual cases from the same state, which both show well how a diagnosis of either mental disease or mental defect must necessarily devalue all behaviour attributed to that cause.

The first is another instance of a woman taken in adultery. It is reported under the heading 'Need of Closer Cooperation between Courts, Psychiatrists, and Social Workers'; no doubt in order to emphasise the distance travelled since New Testament days. The accused 'pleaded guilty, and was sentenced by a district court to six months in the house of correction . . . she was examined, under the Massachusetts law, as to her mental condition. . . .' The appointed experts reported: 'She seemed absolutely without shame in talking of her past; seemed to lack any true sense of moral decency. . . . She could "see no harm in a woman's leading an immoral life unless she bore children". Thought "there was no harm in a woman's supporting herself by that means". According to Binet tests, she graded up to 7.8 years of age. It would seem from this history and from the Binet examination that this woman is a menace to any community in which she might be living. In our opinion she is a suitable case to be committed to a school for the feeble-minded.'[129]

The diagnosis this time was not mental disease but mental deficiency. Yet that makes the example none the less relevant to illustrate the point that to accept any such diagnosis is to commit yourself to construing the consequent verbal behaviour of your patient not as a contribution to discussion but as so much symptomatic utterance. The essential nature of this clinical posture comes out in a manifesto by a leading British Freudian. We must leave till Part III questions about the self-destructive epistemological rashness of his statement: 'The analyst must above all be an analyst. That is to say he must know positively that all human emotional reactions, all human judgements, and even reason itself, are but the tools of the unconscious; and that such seemingly acute convictions which an intelligent person like this possesses are but the inevitable effect of causes which lie buried in the unconscious levels of his psyche.'[130]

Had the Massachusetts experts been prepared instead to listen to this supposedly feeble-minded prostitute as a person, they could scarcely have failed to notice that their own chosen quotations provide no evidence whatsoever of either incompetence or fecklessness. On the contrary indeed: for, although square parents like myself would hate to see our own daughters adopt such a way of life,[131] it cannot be denied that any prostitute provides – in the strongest sense – a public service; while this particular woman displayed a responsible attitude to procreation contrasting most favourably with the doctrinaire fecklessness then and still encouraged by the laws of her state.

The second case is that of James Cooper. On 20 April 1957 he went to the apartment of his former fiancée Connie Gilman. Before ringing the bell he took care to release the safety catch of his automatic. When she came to the door, he fired nine shots into her; which performance was, to no one's surprise, instantly fatal. Cooper then went to the police to give himself up. Asked whether he fired with intent to kill, he said: 'I fired to blow her fucking head off. How many times do you want me to tell you?'[132]

The point about this forthright if somewhat coarse-spoken young man was that, having done what he did, after full deliberation, intentionally, and in the execution carefully, he then most resolutely and inflexibly insisted that just this was what he had done. Against every pressure from both the defence counsel and the officers of the Commonwealth he rejected the suggestion that he was or had been mentally diseased, and hence in some relevant way incapable: incontinent, that is, in the sense in which this is an infantile or a senile rather than a playboy characteristic. In his final address to the court he spoke with a direct and lucid brevity, which the expert witnesses ought to have envied: 'It is my opinion that any decision other than guilty, guilty of murder in the first degree, with no recommendation for leniency, is [*sic*] a miscarriage of justice.'

The jury agreed. The judge passed sentence of electrocution. But there were those who persisted in denying Cooper's right to his own action, and to its legal consequences. Eventually they succeeded in drumming up sufficient psychiatric opinion to secure commutation to life imprisonment. Cooper then hanged himself. No doubt this enabled Massachusetts to have the last word: to insist – in impious perjury – that the balance of his mind must therefore have been disturbed; and thus to do what it still could to deprive Cooper posthumously of the dignity of his final protest.

The first of these two cases – like that, in the previous section, of the supposed paranoiac – underlined the point that a diagnosis of mental disease, whether correct or incorrect, and hence whether rightly or wrongly, requires that we discount as merely symptomatic the consequent verbal behaviour of the patient. This second case brings out that the same diagnosis similarly requires that all consequent behaviour be discounted. It is not really the conduct of a person. It is, rather, something which happens to a patient. These dehumanising implications are very serious. So it is correspondingly important neither to make nor to endorse the sort of diagnosis which warrants them save where it in its turn is fully justified.

Of course there are situations in which there may be more or less good and perhaps sufficient reasons for giving or seeking a false diagnosis. In many jurisdictions for instance it may be necessary for a woman who wants a legal abortion somehow to persuade a psychiatrist to certify that to have the baby would gravely damage her mental health. I cannot wish to discourage either the disingenuous or the ingenuous exploitation of loopholes in such bad laws. Yet it should be recognised as one more argument for reform that they assume that no woman once pregnant may be excused childbirth duty unless she is, or would become, psychologically incapable of coping.[133] And furthermore even the whitest of white lies is as a lie obnoxious.

What appears to be more common is the rendering of dubious diagnoses for even more dubious political purposes. Dr Thomas Szasz has offered good reason for challenging the verdicts of mental disability handed down in the cases of David Pratt and Ezra Pound.[134] The former was the gentleman farmer who assassinated Dr Hendrik Verwoerd, Prime Minister of

South Africa. The latter was an American poet who during
the Second World War made broadcasts from Rome under the
auspices of his admired friend Benito Mussolini. In each case it
is easy to see why the very different authorities involved should
have wished to avoid the embarrassments of public trials,
possibly followed by executions; especially when this could be
done by means which simultaneously discredited the awkward
idea that Pratt and Pound might have acted from conviction.

The most recent, the most numerous, and perhaps the most
flagrant examples are however to be found in the Soviet Union.
Here the primary intention to discredit dissidents, especially
the more talented, is made manifest in the measures to secure
the complicity of the victims. Where in the more murderous
1930s the NKVD was charged with extorting confessions of
premeditated and sustained counter-revolutionary activity,
its latest successor, the KGB, may insist that if the patient's
sentence is to have an end he must first admit that his dangerous
thoughts or his brave deeds were the outcome of some mental
disability. Thus the geophysicist Nikolai Nikolayevich Sam-
sonov was required, and eventually compelled, to admit that
he was of unsound mind when he wrote his letter maintaining
that it was really Stalin himself who between 1934 and 1937
effected a counter-revolutionary coup. So too the medical
establishment of the Leningrad Special Psychiatric Hospital –
wholly emancipated from un-Leninist Hippocratic inhibitions
– have in their zeal to secure the desired recantation threatened
to employ aminazin (adding, considerately, that this could not
but aggravate their patient's real disease of the liver).[135]

Enough has surely been said in previous sections about the
general wrongness of making your criterion for mental disease,
not some sort of incapacity to behave, but actual disfavoured
behaviour. But more needs to be made of the particular case
where the incapacity in question is supposed to be a defect of
reason.

One difficulty, which has been touched already at the end
of Section 10 of the present Part II, is that we speak of what a
man wants as reasons for his acting to satisfy these wants.
It can thus seem that anyone whose desires are not our desires
must when he acts be by that token acting without reason.
If we are not to build into our concept of mental disease
requirements of conformity, the only solution is to refuse to

accept that mere deviance in wants constitutes mental incapacity. It may be that through this and similar refusals we shall be opening a gap between the concept of mental disease, developed upon the analogy with physical disease, and the much older notions of insanity and madness. Yet this cannot be an objection. For it has always been obvious that even the most ungenerous employers of the expression 'mental disease' have been willing to apply it to many cases which were not cases of insanity. So the only possibly new point is that there may be some examples of insanity which are not examples of mental disease.[136]

For the same good nonconformist reason we must reject the suggestion, entertained in Section 4 of Part I, that extreme imprudence might be taken in itself as a sign of psychological disorder. For, in so far as prudence is a matter of both sound calculation and studious pursuit of one's own interests, any disinterested sacrifice must be imprudent. It was certainly in the last degree imprudent for Muscovite dissidents to demonstrate in Red Square against the 1968 reconquest of Czechoslovakia. But since they did this with their eyes open, knowing exactly what they were letting themselves in for, it would be not just mistaken but indecent to put down their principled bravery to a defect of reason.

The same argument of course applies equally to less admirable figures. In Part v of *The Civilization of the Renaissance in Italy* Jacob Burkhardt describes: 'The thirst for blood on its own account, the devilish delight in destruction . . . clearly exemplified in . . . Caesar Borgia, whose cruelties were certainly out of all proportion to the ends they had in view. In Sigismondo Malatesta, tyrant of Rimini, the same disinterested love of evil may be detected. It is not only the Court of Rome, but the verdict of history which convicts him of murder, rape, adultery, incest, sacrilege, perjury and treason, committed not once but often.'

At a less splendid level, the fact that George Smith offered as his only reason for attempting to strangle a stranger the inadequate avowal 'I wanted her necklace for my girl', is no reason for attributing to him any defect of reason. But that he was indeed thus defective begins to emerge when we learn of his 'leaning a long ladder against the glass of the big window in the third floor classroom, about to climb up it to see over the wall of the factory building next door, and failing to realise that the window would have broken and thrown him down three storeys to the school yard'.[137] He himself seems to have appreciated this and other similarly unrecognised dangers once his attention had been officiously drawn to them.

That last point is important. For we are in trouble the moment any possibly disputatious vagary of belief is conscripted to serve as the crucial criterion. We have to know: first that the beliefs in question – unlike the 'paranoiac delusions' of Stephen Dennison – really are without foundation; and second and much trickier that for the subject to persist in them is to march well outside the undemarcated frontier of ordinarily human cognitive fallibility. Whatever else may be unsure or indeterminate here, it is clear that to fulfil this special function the delusion must be subject to fairly direct and indisputably decisive disconfirmation. There is perhaps no restriction other than the requirement of erroneousness on the possible content of delusions as such. But if we are to treat the diagnosis of mental disease with the caution which the seriousness of its implications demands, only peculiarly flagrant kinds can serve as criteria. Most certainly it will not do to rest your case upon such essentially ideological phenomena as the 'obsessive reformist delusions' of the subject.[138] It is wrong in general to take even an erroneous belief if not wholly indefensible as the criterion of the presence of mental disease. The offence is compounded in those particular cases where this is done precisely in order that the diagnosis shall then in turn serve to discredit the believer himself and, indirectly, his belief.[139]

To all such attempts to misemploy the dangerous but necessary notion of mental disease some angry words of Freud constitute a proper answer. His biographer mentions a first grim medical report upon the development of Freud's cancer: 'Many years later . . . I told him that we had discussed whether or not to inform him. . . with blazing eyes he asked: "Mit welchem Recht?" ' – by what right?[140]

III Determinist Presuppositions Cannot Disprove

I   Part II examined the notions of 'Disease and Mental Disease'; and tried, among other things, to establish some paradigms of what can and cannot be properly so described. It may be objected that there are many actual and possible intermediate cases in which, even where the clinical facts were not in dispute, it would upon the principles there indicated be difficult to decide whether or not to diagnose mental disease. That is surely true. But it is also in such matters what is always to be expected. The present essay cannot hope to be more than introductory, and the only sensible way to begin is by first getting clear about the extremes and the principles. For the extremes are what the marginal cases are intermediate between, and it is of the general principles that the application problems are application problems.

A far more serious objection is that the fundamental conceptions in terms of which I have tried to distinguish mental disease from mental health are pre- or even anti-scientific. All of what little space remains must be devoted to this challenge: 'Free will – to a lawyer – is not a philosophical theory or a religious concept or a scientific hypothesis. It is a given, a basic assumption in legal theory and practice. To the psychiatrist, this position is preposterous; he seeks a clear operational definition of "free" and of "will".'[141]

These words come from Dr Karl Menninger's onslaught on *The Crime of Punishment*. More significant, because reluctant, is a statement made by Dr C. Ounsted of the Park Hospital for Children, Headington, Oxford. He made it just after suggesting – a brave and lonely voice in a colloquium of orthopsychiatrists! – that children need, and even wish, to be treated as accountable; and hence, on occasion, punished: 'The legal system is based on the notion of freewill (illusion though it may be) and we deny it at our peril. Although I hold that this notion must be excluded from any scientific discourse, freewill forms the only rock on which a sane structure of civil and criminal law can be built. It underlies the law of contract as much as it justifies the demand of "Guilty or Not Guilty" in criminal cases.'[142] To complete the trio, the author of the book, *Delinquency and Human Nature*, discussed in Section 4 of Part I, insists: 'Now I am well aware of a very natural feeling that every delinquent is not "a psychological case". From a broad social point of view it would not be healthy for bad behaviour to be popularly regarded, and excused, as symptomatic of psychological disorder. But the most commonplace of acts can be shown to be the outcome of many years of complicated causation.'[143]

The challenge can be met; and met too in such a way as to ease fears of general ruin were the actual scientific truth to be disloyally leaked. The key is to start by attending to certain differences, which are inescapably familiar to all human beings in their daily experience; and then to distinguish these in theoretically and evaluatively neutral terms. They are, the differences between motions and movings, as distinguished in Section 4 of Part II. That some of our movements are in this sense movings is a fact so familiar and so undeniable that anything truly irreconcilable with it must for that reason alone be forthwith rejected. It cannot be undermined or overthrown – as David Hume in his first *Inquiry* said of another distinction in the same context – 'by any philosophical theory or speculation whatsoever.' (VIII (ii))

The idea of movings, as opposed to motions, is essential to the concept of action; which, as we saw in Section 15 of Part II, is itself involved in both terms of the untechnical distinction between acting under compulsion and acting of one's own freewill. There is no difficulty at all in providing Dr Menninger with the down-to-earth explanation which he demands. His very words 'operational definitions' refer to possible movings (or not movings); just as much as did his incautious reference elsewhere – 'quasi ipsa veritate coactus': as if compelled by truth herself – to the realities of widespread sexual abstinence.[144] It is furthermore just worth pointing out, with no particular reference to Dr Menninger, how peculiarly reckless it would be for any Freudian psychoanalyst to deny the reality of movings, and whatever else this may involve. For, as we saw in Section

9 of Part II, the distinction between the disease and the cure in the area in which, supposedly, 'our therapy celebrates its triumphs' has to be explicated by reference to precisely this familiar and undeniable difference between motions and movings. The immediate consequence is that, if and in so far as 'freewill' is to be defined in terms of capabilities of moving, Dr Johnson was certainly half right when he said: 'We know our will is free, and there's an end on't.'[145]

★

2 But Dr Johnson was half wrong too. For thus simply to insist upon the basic facts cannot be the end of the affair. We have to go on to ask what they presuppose and imply, and what individual and social significance ought to be accorded to them. One first thing to notice is that these consequent inquiries are badly obstructed by various extraoi dinary, and yet extraordinarily common, misuses and misunderstandings of quite ordinary non-technical terms.

Thus for instance J. B. S. Haldane wrote in his Foreword to Dr J. Lange's *Crime as Destiny*: 'To sum up – an analysis of thirteen cases shows not the faintest evidence of freedom of the will in the ordinary sense of the word. . . . Taking the record of any criminal, we could predict the behaviour of a monozygotic twin placed in the same environment.'[146] But Haldane here is not using the word in its ordinary but in the technical, philosophically libertarian, sense; in which it implies, by definition, uncaused causes and unpredictability in principle. In the ordinary sense, in which freewill is opposed to compulsion, my ability to predict that Haldane would – with certain possible exceptions – follow any instructions of the Communist Party, had no tendency to show that his allegiance was not freely undertaken, freely continued, and, in the end, freely and most honourably abandoned. Nor does any of Dr Lange's evidence of remarkable similarities between the lives of identical twins suggest that these twins were not – in the sense of 'free' indicated in the final paragraph of the previous Section I – free.

Again, in arguing for 'the assumption of an absolute psychic determinism', Freud himself mistakes it that he has to deny that anyone acts 'of his own freewill, and without motives'. So, incredibly, he asserts: 'for some time I have been aware that it is impossible to think of a number, or even of a name, of one's own freewill'.[147] Dr A. A. Brill, his American translator, writes similarly: 'The rank and file of psychiatrists believe in absolute determinism'; and Brill takes this to be antithetical to the belief of 'most persons' that 'they can do what they want, and regardless of motives'.[148] But neither in the ordinary nor even surely in the technical sense does freewill negative motivation. Certainly that I voted, or married, freely and not under compulsion, does not show that I did not do the one because I wanted to keep the other lot out, or the other because I wanted to be married to this one.

Dr Ernest Jones, a member of Freud's Inner Circle and his future biographer, observes: 'that a man's belief in freewill seems to be stronger in proportion to the unimportance of the decision. Everyone is convinced that he is free to choose whether to stand or to sit at a given moment, to cross his right leg over his left or vice versa "as he wishes". With vital decisions on the other hand, it is characteristic that he feels irresistibly impelled towards one and one only, and that he really has no choice in the matter nor desires to have any.'[149]

Suppose we waive the purely psychological point that what is said about vital decisions is not in fact true, since all too many of us find the important ones very difficult indeed. Admittedly it does not inspire confidence when experts tell us about their own areas of specialisation what we as laymen know to be false. But there are two more philosophical immediate objections. First, that some choice was for the chooser so easy that he felt no anguish of decision, does not even begin to show that there were no alternatives for the choice to be between. Existential agonies are therefore not essential. Second, that everyone knew which, given a choice, I would choose, does not make it a whit less true that, when I was given a choice, and then chose as expected, I did in fact choose; choosing whatever I did choose. Foreknowledge not merely does not, but cannot, destroy its object.[150]

These comparatively superficial confusions mask a more fundamental error about the nature of desire. Dr Ernest Jones, like so many others, speaks of a man's own strongest desires as if these were, typically, both compulsions and irresistible: 'It is characteristic that he feels irresistibly impelled towards one and one only'. But this is diametrically wrong. It is wrong in the first place because, as we saw in Section 15 of Part II, to act under compulsion is to be induced by some sort of threat from outside to do what, if only the circumstances were different, you would much rather not do. To assimilate doing what you most want to do to this case is therefore literally preposterous.

In the second place, and more subtly, it is wrong because it construes our desires as overwhelming forces. It is no doubt not despite, but because of, this suggestion that the term 'drive' appeals so strongly to mechanically minded and theoretically ambitious psychologists. For it is far easier to appreciate the ineptness of such a mechanical model if we continue to talk colloquially about what people very much want. It is inept because there is a fundamental difference: between on the one hand explaining that he is lying in the road because he was knocked down, and out, by a wildly driven Austin; and on the other hand explaining that he is lying in the road, more aggressive than helpless, to protest automotive pollution.

In the former case he really is the victim of external forces. In the latter he as surely is not. For, granted that I have a desire for Cynthia, it is no more inevitable that I will set about trying to get her than it follows necessarily that any attempts I do make will succeed. Suppose that some super-psychologist happens to be able to predict both that I will, and that they will. Still all that follows from this alone is, uninterestingly, that I will and that they will; not that I will, inevitably and willy-nilly, nor that they will, irresistibly.[151] Since to do anything surely involves movings (or not movings), and not just motions (or not motions); it must follow that for me to do something because I want to do it does not preclude, but presupposes, that in some relevant sense there are alternatives. So when Luther says – not being paralysed, but as an agent – 'Here I stand. I can no other', it has to be true that in some deeper sense it would have been false to say, 'I can no other.'

A corollary of this understanding of the explanation of human conduct in terms of desires is that Freud's psychic determinism cannot have the implications which he and others have attributed to it. For the essence of this psychic determinism is the claim that whatever is so determined can be explained in terms of motives, plans, desires, purposes, intentions and so on: if not conscious ones then unconscious. Yet – at least as regards the conscious – any explanation of this distinctively human kind does not preclude but presupposes that those concerned, in the deeper sense, could have done otherwise. If in truth they could not, then there was no true action; and all reference to their desires, their plans, their purposes and so forth as its explanation must be without foundation. The perhaps surprising moral is that if universal general Determinism really is, as it is so often assumed to be, incompatible with this fundamental notion of an agent necessarily being able to do otherwise, then psychic determinism is not a particular case of such general Determinism. On the contrary: on any such Incompatibilist assumption psychic determinism must itself be incompatible with general Determinism. We not merely are not, we cannot be, puppets on the strings of our desires.[152]

★

3   But what now of general Determinism, construed as the thesis that the existence of every being and the occurrence of every event have causally sufficient conditions? It is presumably for this rather than for psychic determinism that 'the rank and file of psychiatrists' would opt if they were to realise that they might have to choose. 'Legally', in the words of one who technically is a psychologist rather than a medically qualified psychiatrist, 'the notion of freewill, responsibility, intent and so on, plays a large part in the assessment of culpability. . . . ' However the 'deduction which may be made from our general theory is . . . uncompromising. We would regard behaviour from a completely deterministic point of view; that is to say, the individual's behaviour is determined completely by his heredity and by the environmental influences which have been brought to bear on him. Therefore, to attribute to different individuals, greater or lesser degrees of responsibility seems, from this point of view, a rather meaningless procedure.'[153]

Certainly if we take it, as too many even of those who as philosophers are paid to know better do take it, that the philosophically libertarian is the only relevant sense of 'freewill'; then quite obviously any such Freewill and a universal general Determinism must be incompatible. In that case there would be no philosophical problem; only the question whether Freewill, in that sense, is in fact an actual phenomenon. But, as was seen again in the previous two sections, there are at least two other surely relevant senses; and it is irrefragably certain – certain beyond any possibility of upset by any other discoveries, whether in psychology, or in physiology or even in theology – that in both these senses freewill is a reality.

For it is just not on to contend that there are no such things as movings, as opposed to motions; where both terms are defined, as they were defined in Section 4 of Part II, exclusively by reference to utterly familiar differences. Exactly the same applies to actions done of one's own freewill rather than under compulsion, intentionally rather than unintentionally, and so on; always assuming of course that these pairs of contrasting words or expressions may be interpreted similarly as referring only to the corresponding utterly familiar differences. So, when someone is determined to inform us that his speciality either has shown or presupposes that these realities are not realities, we can know without further inquiry that either his speciality is unsoundly founded or he has misread its implications.[154]

The best hope for the radical wanting to overwhelm this conservative entrenchment is to call out Dr Harvey Cushing's demonstration. That is formidable because it suggests that there are physiological sufficient conditions: not only of our motions, which nobody would want to deny; but also of our movings, which is exactly what many have thought could not be the case. Descartes for instance, although he also wanted for theological reasons to deny the conclusion, maintained – to put it in our terms – that libertarian freewill is an immediate inference from the capacity for movings or not movings.[155] But, whether or not in fact it is or can be established that there are physiological sufficient conditions of our movings, it is surely at least not self-contradictory to suggest that there might be. And furthermore, supposing the inference were indeed sound, the same argument would also constitute a disproof of the existence of the God of traditional theism – the all-knowing, all-powerful, sustaining cause of all creation. Which was of course why Descartes wanted to deny as well as to assert its conclusion.

So suppose instead that some physiologist is able to bring about in someone else: not merely a motion – as the doctor by a well-aimed tap elicits the knee-jerk reflex; but even a moving – in which the subject has 'a full sense that he is voluntarily performing the action'. Clearly, even when this is done – as by the properly scrupulous Dr Cushing – 'with the consent of a patient', the doctor must have some share, along with the patient, in

responsibility for the consequent action. If and when such manipulation is performed either without the knowledge and consent
of the patient or actually against his wishes, then it is hard indeed to see how he, rather than his manipulator, can properly
be held in any degree responsible for the behaviour resulting.

Yet it seems that precisely this would be our universal human
condition if traditional theism were the truth. Nor is the idea
that this is its implication peculiar to Calvin and to those other
theologians whom we are all taught to call predestinarian. The
same substance is found in many others, however great the
differences in tone of voice and in frankness of expression. Always one of the frankest, and always the most vigorous, Luther
argues: 'Natural reason itself . . . would be forced by the conviction of its own judgement to concede this much, even if no
Scripture existed. For all men find the following convictions
written in their hearts . . . ; first, that God is omnipotent, not
only in power but also in action . . . ; second, that He Knows
and foreknows, and can neither err nor be deceived. These two
points being allowed . . . they are at once compelled by irrefut-
able logic to admit that we are not made by our own will . . .
and accordingly that we do not do anything by right of "freewill", but according to what God foreknew and works by his
infallible and immutable counsel and power.'[156]

The crux for us is that by 'freewill' Luther means always
libertarian freewill. What he says makes it perfectly clear that,
while God always fixes all human choices, and while there is
therefore no place in God's creation for libertarian freewill,
this in no way prejudices the reality of freewill in our two other
senses. Thus he raises, but forthwith drops, the question: 'Why
then does He not alter those evil wills which He moves? This
question touches the secrets of His Majesty, where "His judgements are past finding out" [cf. *Romans*, XI, 33].'[157] But elsewhere Luther insists: ' . . . I did not say "of compulsion" . . . a
man without the Spirit of God does not do evil against his will,
under pressure, as though he were taken by the scruff of his
neck and dragged into it, like a thief or a footpad being dragged
off against his will to punishment: but he does it spontaneously
and voluntarily.'[158]

Since the arch-Protestant Luther, like his Roman Catholic
opponents, believed that most of God's human creatures would
be condemned to unending torture; and since, as both parties

also believed, God had arranged that this would be the consequence of choices made in senses which Luther clearly saw that the same God must also arrange; how can we fail to be pierced by his heartcry? For, seeing no way to escape the proposition that we are the creatures of such a Creator, Luther concludes: that 'the highest degree of faith is to believe that He is merciful, though He saves so few and damns so many; to believe that He is just, though of His own will He makes us perforce proper subjects for damnation, and seems (in the words of Erasmus) "to delight in the torments of poor wretches and to be a fitter object for hate than for love". If I could by any means understand how this same God . . . can yet be merciful and just, there would be no need for faith.'[159]

★

4   For us the reason for quoting Luther is to bring out as clearly and as dramatically as possible three points. First no discovery, simply as an unapplied discovery – not even the most supercosmic discovery – could ever abolish familiar differences, or invalidate distinctions founded solely upon such differences. Second the reality of freewill in both the two senses thus defined constitutes no warrant for assuming the reality of freewill in the technical libertarian sense; and hence, conversely, the manifest irreconcilability with that of general Determinism provides no reason at all for assuming that whatever presupposes or implies this kind of Determinism can have no room for either of the other two more homely sorts of freewill. Third, although discoveries cannot simply abolish familiar differences they may well demand some revision, or even revolution, in ideas about the significance of those differences.

More must now be said, with special reference to an atheist general Determinism, about points two and three. Against two it may be objected that, although the words 'moving' and 'motion' were given their special new senses by reference only to observed differences this does not apply to 'freewill' as opposed to 'compulsion', to 'intentional' as contrasted with 'unintentional' or to the members of any other pairs of contrasting colloquial terms for characterising actions. It remains possible therefore that any or all of these other terms, so vital to the assessment of responsibility, are, like the term 'lunatic' as employed in the days of Sir Matthew Hale, partly descriptive and partly theoretical. Just as he and his contemporaries when they used the word 'lunatic' were both labelling the phenomena and venting their theory that these were controlled by the phases of the moon, so it might be argued that both they and we in employing certain of those other terms are both indicating directly observable differences, and committing ourselves to the hypothesis that we have here a case of libertarian freewill: 'We use the word "free" not simply to characterise a certain class of actions which we could, so to speak, pick out by eye, but rather to say of those actions that no complete causal account can be given of them.'[160]

It is unfortunate that, even among trained professional philosophers, spokesmen for this kind of thesis so often write as if they had never heard of the notion that, in ordinary untechnical usage, the expression 'of my own freewill' refers to the absence not of causes but of compulsion.[161] To anyone seized of this elementary and by now hackneyed truth the best bet would seem to be to urge that it is the general idea of action, rather than the particular case of acting without compulsion, which embraces (the possibility of) uncaused causes; causes, that is, with posterity but without ancestors.

Even this best bet however is still not good. For the claim will presumably have to rest on giving a libertarian interpretation to that 'deeper sense in which it would have been false' for Luther, or for any other agent, 'to say. "I can no other" '. Suppose now that we have appreciated that there is at least no inconsistency in saying that God – or even Dr Harvey Cushing – can manipulate a man's movings and not movings. Then it surely becomes in the last degree implausible to suggest that, while the 'could have done otherwise' which can be defined by reference to the observed differences between movings and motions does not of course carry any implications about uncaused causes, the 'could have done otherwise' which is essential to the concept of action is quite different; because this one, unlike the other, does presuppose libertarian freewill.

One simple but important reason why it is so easy to reach such implausible conclusions lies in a widespread failure to appreciate the difference: between on the one hand appealing directly to established correct usage as the determinant of the meaning of a word; and on the other hand requesting people to report what they themselves believe its meaning to be. If for instance you ask a group of philosophical beginners to spell out the meaning of the word 'mind', then the chances are that most of them will construe it as referring to a kind of logical substances. Yet those same students, reading on the sports pages that 'Ethiopia's win in the marathon was a triumph of mind over matter', will certainly interpret this correctly, as saying no more than some less pretentious alternative mentioning only the tremendous determination shown by the victor. Again they will interpret overheard dons talk about fourth-class minds as referring, not to tawdry spiritual substances, but to the lamentable intellectual incapacities of some of their contemporaries – or of some of their teachers!

So, similarly, if in a philosophical context we ask someone to tell us what he believes that the word 'free' means, then he is all too likely to assert that it is used 'to say of . . . actions that no complete causal account can be given of them'. Nevertheless, although there certainly is such a technical libertarian sense of 'freewill', this is, as we have seen, equally certainly not the ordinary sense; the sense in which in his philosophically unselfconscious moments even our respondent himself would use the word.

Yet it is precisely ordinary as opposed to technical senses with which we need to be primarily concerned. For the fundamental ideas of moral and legal accountability are themselves ordinary and philosophically non-technical, and they are logically linked with manifold distinctions drawn in a correspondingly ordinary and correspondingly non-technical vocabulary. In so far as these distinctions are rooted in familiar differences, and in so far as the words and expressions used to mark these undoubted differences carry no theoretical load, then they cannot be impugned by any discovery whatsoever, whether scientific or theological. So freewill in the technical, philosophically libertarian, sense becomes relevant only if and where it can be shown to be presupposed by, or encapsulated in, some of the crucial ordinary ideas. Where, but only where, this can be done, there, but only there, is general Determinism as such a threat – or a promise.

About this all that I can reasonably hope, and have tried, to do here is: first to show that it must not be taken as axiomatic that it is libertarian freewill, a notion which no doubt 'must be excluded from any scientific discourse', which 'forms the only rock on which a sane structure of civil and criminal law can be built'; and second to suggest that there are some good reasons for believing that this putative axiom is in fact false.

The third lesson which the consideration of Luther can underline is that, although familiar differences cannot be abolished by discoveries, such discoveries may sometimes demand some revision in accepted ideas about the significance of those differences. Suppose with Luther we learn, or imagine that we have learnt, that we are all of us creatures of a cosmic Cushing: 'He's got the whole world in His hands.' Certainly we must now abandon any terms involving libertarian freewill: that notion can in such a universe have no application. But equally certainly, as Luther also insisted, all the familiar observed differences must remain altogether unchanged. Sometimes a man will be seen to act 'spontaneously and voluntarily'. Sometimes he will act 'against his will under pressure'. And sometimes he may be 'taken by the scruff of his neck and dragged'. Yet for all that, as with a candour rare among theologians Luther himself again makes clear, the significance of these differences cannot remain exactly what it was before. For now we see that 'of His own will he makes us perforce proper subjects for damnation.'

It is no part of our present business to pursue the extremely hard question of exactly how and where such an appalling theological discovery ought to change our ideas. It is sufficient to appreciate: first, in general, that a radical reassessment would be required; and second, in particular, that it must be absurd and outrageous for the Supreme Judge to base discriminations upon those differences which would concern a human court. For, whereas the prisoners in any wordly dock are beings independent of their judges, creatures have all and only those characteristics fixed by their Creator.[162]

Suppose now instead that what we are accepting is an atheist and mortalist Determinism. Suppose too that this view does not after all preclude the possibility of action. Then it is at least not obvious that any general revision is required; although of course those holding particular contrary philosophical beliefs will need to change. For, upon the Compatibilist assumption stated, there will be no call to detheoreticise the meanings of any everyday terms: as the advance of psychiatry surely required the detheoreticisation of the term 'lunatic'; and as the Copernican Revolution certainly would have required that of the expression 'The sun is rising' if previously that really was – as everyone else says it was – theoretically loaded. Nor, upon that same assumption, will it be clear that 'The issue of . . . determinism, albeit a metaphysical, not a scientific and operational problem, is basic to the entire controversy that has raged between the law and psychiatry, the law and other disciplines.' For no reason will have been given to doubt the classical assumption: 'To assert that man is a free moral agent, capable of choosing right from wrong . . . engaging in rational voluntaristic conduct, is classical criminology.'[163]

It is here neither possible nor necessary to investigate the implications of Determinism thoroughly. But three further short suggestions may be useful. The first is that it is as wrong as it is common to confound the two doctrines just now treated in succession. The crucial difference is that in the former, the theist, there is another agent either to share or to monopolise responsibility; whereas in the latter, the atheist, there is not. Thus it will not do, here any more than anywhere else, to argue directly from possibility to actuality: to urge for example that because the Cushing demonstration perhaps shows that all my movings could in principle be produced by the manipulation of someone else; therefore I always in fact am being thus manipulated, albeit perhaps by ongoings in my own central nervous system. Nor will it do, notwithstanding that it is forever being done, first to personify Fate or the Unconscious or Heredity or what have you, and then to draw conclusions from your own fictions which would be justified only if these were facts.

The second suggestion is that we must never forget that we are beings of flesh and blood: that our brains for instance are somehow parts of us; and not of an external world around us. It is therefore absurd to speak of 'the relation of personality to the body we inherit'.[164] Nor, since we are thus rational animals, can it be right to take physiological accounts of what goes on when I argue for some conclusion, or decide to perform some action, as precluding the possibilities, that I have good reasons for what I am saying, and that I shall do what I shall do because I want to. If this is so, and it surely is, than it must be wrong to say: 'If human actions were completely explicable according to a physical scheme of explanation, then they could not really be explained according to a rational or human scheme of explanation'; and wrong too to take Determinism to be self-discrediting on the grounds that the Determinist 'does not hold his Determinist views because they are true, but because he has such-and-such a genetic make-up, and has received such-and-such stimuli'.[165]

Again it must be similarly wrong: first to define 'the freedom of the will' to mean 'the capacity to make and execute choices that are essentially conditioned by conscious desire to achieve a certain envisaged end . . . to make purposive choices among alternatives and to direct action in accordance with such choices'; and then after that to regard it as an open question 'whether human beings have any real capacity to initiate sequences or to break into causal chains by an effort of will'.[166] For, since there can be no doubt whatsoever but that people do frequently intervene to prevent developments which certainly would have occurred but for their intervention, the only possible remaining question is whether people – considered now, wrongly, as incorporeal Cartesian subjects of consciousness – are or are not able to inhibit or to trigger mechanisms in those organisms in which they, as it were, reside.

The third suggestion is very pedestrian. Yet pedestrians do have their feet on the ground. The suggestion is that we never forget that you do not have to be an uncaused cause to be a cause. So it is, simply, wrong to say that, on Determinist assumptions, 'his action did not really depend on him, but was determined by antecedent external circumstances'; and also, but more subtly, wrong to say that 'if I am determined, my will can be left out of consideration as an independent factor, because it can be calculated from other factors already given.'[167] It is ridiculous thus to assume that nothing can really depend on anything which is in turn dependent upon something else. This would imply that no causal chain could consist of more than one link. Yet I am none the less a father for having had one.

★

5   Determinism has been considered so far in Part III as the ground for the objection 'that the fundamental conceptions in terms of which I have tried to distinguish mental disease from mental health are pre- or even anti-scientific'. The response has been: first to outline what Hume in his first *Inquiry* called a 'reconciling project' (VIII (i)); and second to threaten – if noth-

ing along these lines proves acceptable – totally to turn the tables.

It is impossible here to do more than first sketch how such a project might be developed, and then indicate that the weight not only of philosophical but also of theological opinion appears to have been in this sense Compatibilist. Heaven forbid any attempt to settle a philosophical question by a headcount of authorities. Yet some attention does have to be paid to tradition if the arguments offered are to be given due consideration. The threat too is important. There are some things which we cannot accept from experts. If it really is either a presupposition or a finding of the psychological sciences that there are no such things as movings, only motions; and that all these familiar distinctions made by reference to the differences between what we can and what cannot do at will, properly belong with such garbage ideas as witchcraft or phlogiston: then, without any doubt whatever, it is the pretensions of these sciences which must be rejected, not the inexpugnable realities of everyday life. If this really is the presupposition or the implication, the which I do not believe, then it is absurd for Stott to preen himself upon public-spiritedly soft-pedalling a truth which 'from a broad social point of view' it would not be healthy to have noised abroad among the lower orders. For, on this assumption, the scandal would be the scandal of psychology itself; and 'the rabble without doors' would have good reason to ridicule a kind of learning which would deny the undeniable.[168]

Two other lines of thought must be at least indicated before we stop. The first is that one must not appeal to general Determinism to establish only the relatively particular conclusion that all crime is in fact an expression of mental disease. For this absolutely universal premise cannot be thus conveniently controlled: if the Incompatibilists are right what it threatens is, as was suggested in Section 13 of Part II, total categorial catastrophe.

Lombroso quotes an eighteenth-century source: 'Rondeau, governor under Joseph II'. In his *Essai physique sur la peine du mort* this Rondeau maintained: 'Crime does not exist in nature; it is the law alone which imposes this unjust designation on acts which are necessary and inevitable. . . . Anger is a passing fever, jealousy a momentary delirium, the rapacity of the thief and swindler a momentary disease, and the depraved passions which drive men to sins against nature are organic imperfections. . . .

The murderer himself is a sick man like other criminals . . . the moment all crime is recognised as the natural product and logical consequence of some disease, punishment must become only a medical treatment.'[169]

In the first half of our own century the American attorney Clarence Darrow became notorious for securing acquittals in murder cases by appeals to universal Determinism; although it is surely significant that he made no such appeal in the great 'Monkey Trial', defending a man who had in a Bible Belt public school taught the theory of evolution by natural selection. Darrow claimed generally: 'There is now no room for such a doctrine as freedom of the will. Nothing in the universe is outside the law, whether mineral, vegetable, or animal'. So it is apparently clear that 'crime is a disease whose root is in heredity and environment.' The same arbitrary selectivity shows again when Darrow continues: 'The transgression of organised society in the treatment of crime would not be so great if . . . scientists had not long since found the cause of crime. . . . These students have pointed the way for the treatment of the disease.'[170]

Now obviously, if we may validly argue from such Determinism to the conclusion that criminal behaviour cannot be controllable, then, by parity of reasoning, we may also argue that from the same premise it follows that all behaviour whatsoever must be similarly uncontrollable. But this conclusion wreaks havoc with, among many others, the concepts of mental disease and mental health. For it wholly destroys the crucial distinction: between how a man actually behaves, whether in movings or in motions; and how he could have behaved, in alternative movings or not movings. Where – one is tempted to say – no one is ever capable of doing or not doing anything at will, there indeed everyone must be in some way 'sick, sick, sick'. Yet even this is misleading. For the situation envisaged is: not one where everyone happens to have got the same disease simultaneously, although all or some will hopefully sometime recover; but one where it would be physically impossible for the idea of a cure ever to find any proper application at all. We should therefore be reduced to a position far more absurd than that of the nineteenth-century psychiatrist John Haslam who, to the great irritation of the court, once deposed: 'I never saw any human being who was of sound mind.'[171]

Of course no one would accept such a crazy position once he

had seen what it involved. The danger is that those who believe that these are the true consequences of Deterministic truth will take this as a reason: not, as it is, for revising their ideas about Determinism; but, as it is not, for challenging the basis of the sort of understanding of mental health and mental disease developed in Part II. Favoured and disfavoured behaviour as such are then all too likely to become the criteria of, respectively, mental health and mental disease. But, since it will surely still be assumed that the patient is necessarily a victim, it will as before appear obvious that it must be in his interests to be straightened – that this must in truth be what he himself really wants. (When the metaphysician says that this is really that, what he really means is that it is not really.)

There is worse to come. For all ideas of justice surely presuppose accountable agents, for whom this or that treatment would be fair or unfair, or to whom one thing or another is due. In the rather shocking statement quoted in Section 1 of Part 1, Dr Karl Menninger was right at least in so far as he was insisting only on the complete inappositeness of the conception of justice to the determination of the effectiveness of means to cure a disease. A universe in which Determinism is permitted to exclude all possibility of action can therefore offer no purchase to such ideas; and consequently justice could there set no limits to the possibilities of seizing people for the purpose of effecting in them whatever transformations might be adjudged to be socially desirable. Bradley therefore seems to have been substantially right in another harsh characterisation of a contemporary tendency: 'There is a way of thinking and feeling about punishment, not uncommon in our days, which exhibits a high degree of inconsistency. It more or less explicitly accepts the doctrine that crime (all of it or some of it) is mere disease.' Hence, 'Criminals, some or all, are diseased, and are therefore innocent; and the innocent, of course, are by justice proclaimed to be sacred.' For, 'Justice is the assignment of benefit and injury according to desert. . . .' But, Bradley continues, if a 'man is not a moral agent . . . surely what follows is that justice is indifferent to his case. What is just or unjust has surely nothing to do with our disposal of his destiny.' Bradley therefore concludes: 'So long only as we do not pretend retributively to punish him, we may cut him off, if that seems best for the general good.'[172]

*

6   The second further thing to be noticed finally is that the philosophical discussions of the present Part III cannot be dismissed as irrelevant to the practical. For so long as those trained in the psychological disciplines see it, at least in their self-conscious, working hours, as a requirement of their cloth to hold that really there is no such thing as choice, and so on; so long will they find themselves, or be found, misrepresenting their own observations, and making recommendations which are in part vitiated by these professional misconceptions. However much common sense will keep breaking through, and constantly and happily it does, still even the most sensible among them seem to have at least some nagging feeling that really they ought to believe that the power of choice is a chimaera. It is therefore not surprising that hard-headed lawyers and traditionalist plain men should often suspect what is offered to them as psychiatric expertise. Some good may be done here by the sort of superficial diplomacy which repudiates extreme statements as unofficial, and which attempts to demarcate reserved bailiwicks for all parties.[173] But a more direct and radical confrontation is also required. For, though sometimes perhaps exaggerated, the suspicions in this case are well founded.

For example back in Section 4 of Part I we saw Stott concluding that 'delinquent breakdown is an escape from an emotional situation which, for the particular individual with the various conditionings of his background, becomes at least temporarily unbearable.' We noticed that this conclusion was supported by the claim that 'The offender is so patently acting against his own interests'; a claim which in its turn was equally patently not supported by Stott's own evidence. After the additonal quotation given in Section I of Part III it is hard to resist the conjecture that Stott was blinkered by his own apparent metaphysical conviction that every delinquent indeed must be 'a psychological case'; since 'the most commonplace of acts can be shown to be the outcome of many years of complicated causation'.

It is again, I submit, the same misguiding metaphysical belief that ' "what I will not, that I cannot do" ', rather than any empirical facts actually reported, which determined Dr Kate Friedlander's conclusions: 'The scientific facts set out in the preceding chapters go to show that the offender, through no fault of his own, has been unable to build up a character which of itself would enable him to respect the claims of the community and, in certain situations, to regard them as more important than the satisfaction of his own desires. We have also seen, at least by implication, that if we are law-abiding citizens it is merely because we have had the opportunity to become socially adjusted.'[174]

Even that good adjustment still leaves the rest of us a bad lot. Non-offenders, the future Honorary Psychiatrist to the Institute for the Scientific Treatment of Delinquency insists in her Preface, 'feel justified in condemning the behaviour of the offender and pressing for his punishment. They rationalise their attitude on the grounds that they themselves undergo frustrations for the sake of the community, whereas the delinquent gratifies his desires to the discomfort of his fellow citizens.' Wordworth's words apply more widely (*The Excursion*, IV); it is not only self-disparagement which affords

> To meditative spleen a grateful feast

Once more, the same misguiding metaphysical belief led another British Freudian, Dr Charles Berg, to write: 'I am using the word "blame" rather loosely, for psychology does not blame anyone; it recognises that a person's acts, like the acts of any organism or organ, are predetermined by heredity, development, and enviroment.'[175]

Another interesting mistake may be involved in this example, a mistake running parallel to that which certainly is to be found in the passage from the same author quoted in Section 16 of Part II. From the fact that certain terms are not part of the vocabulary of some science, it cannot be concluded that that science shows the illegitimacy of the corresponding notions. That musical and gastronomic characteristics are neglected by physicists in their working hours; and that 'counterpoint' and 'tastiness' do not, therefore, belong to the vocabulary of physics; provides not the slightest reason for saying that physics reveals their unreality. So from the fact, if it is a fact, that a psychologist must not, in his professional capacity, engage in either blame or praise, it does not follow that his discipline has revealed these activities to be without rational foundation.

There is no doubt that Dr Berg did make the parallel mistake in the other case. If 'To achieve success the analyst must above all be an analyst'; if, that is, he must in his analytic hours treat

every utterance by his patients as actually or possibly symptomatic; then it emphatically does not follow that 'he must know
positively that all human emotional reactions, all human judgements and even reason itself, are but the tools of the unconscious.' For the premise here is a modest confession of the calculated limitations of one particular professional interest, whereas the proposed conclusion is to be construed as a piece of
wildly deflationary metaphysics: there just is, it is supposed thus
to have been revealed, no place anywhere for such concepts as
'well-argued case' and 'well-founded assurance'; presumably
not even, we might add nastily, either in or in talk about the
literature of psychoanalysis.

Now it is all very well for Dr Michael Balint, writing 'On
Punishing Offenders', to begin: 'Being a doctor, I propose to
treat criminality as an illness'; and then to try to apply the
notions of morbidity, diagnosis and recovery rate[176]. But it
would be quite a different thing, and quite wrong, to argue:
that because I may or must, for certain limited purposes, treat
this as if it were that; therefore I am assuming, or have even
shown, that this just is that – and that's that.

The temptation here is to confuse statements of particular
professional limitations with appeals to special professional
knowledge. It is fine to say: either 'As a doctor, in his professional capacity that is, he can talk about, has a right to talk
about, only health; and not politics or religion, or the good life
in general'; or 'As a doctor, thanks to his specialised training
that is, he can recognise a case of encephalitis lethargica; and we
cannot, and so must shut up, and leave things to him'. But it is a
very different matter, and no implication of either of these propositions, to say that as a doctor, thanks to his specialised training, he knows that the universe contains nothing but what, as a
doctor, he is supposed to concentrate on in his working hours.

Yet again: the same basic misguiding beliefs about Determinism are surely not only in part consequences but also in part
causes of those extraordinary misunderstandings just now noticed
in Section 2. The result of such endemic confusions about central
elements in the very rich colloquial vocabulary [177] is to make a
century-old comment on Dr Maudsley's *Responsibility in Mental
Disease* even more relevant today than it was then: 'How in the
world is it possible to say what relieves a madman of responsibility, until you know what makes a sane man responsible?'; for

'until we know whether a writer is one with us in our main beliefs as to a sane man's responsibility, how can we . . . receive his evidence as to anyone's non-responsibility, when, so far as we can see, on his showing no one (sane or mad) would be what we call responsible?'[178]

What indeed is the responsibility which, in the view of those for whom Dr Walter Bromberg speaks, we have not got? 'Many psychiatrists feel', he tells us in *Crime and the Mind*, 'that no man can really "choose" a course of conduct, because "free choice" is determined by each individual's cultural and psychological background, his unconscious impulses, identifications, predetermined wishes and drives. Thus a criminal offender cannot be considered psychologically "free" in any absolute sense.' He concludes: 'It is understandable that psychiatrists can look with greater ease on partial responsibility as a defence against criminal responsibility in selected cases, since the traditional view of absolute freewill cannot be supported clinically.'[179]

Really to choose a course of conduct; to be psychologically free in an absolute sense; to have what clinical experience has at last revealed that we do not have: this would apparently be to be without any loyalties or commitments, without any cultural or psychological background. The wholly responsible man would be, if he were, a person without any relevant past. He would have to lack almost everything which constitutes the difference between one individual and another. As Mrs Marmeladov is said to have said: "She can't help herself, I'm afraid. Its her character, you see".'[180]

Notes

Publication details of works cited in the Notes will be found in the Bibliography. Numbers in square brackets relate to authors of whom more than one work is cited.

1. To Albert Hodges, 4 April 1864.

2. The reference is to John Wilson's *Language and the Pursuit of Truth*. What Lady Wootton believes that she learnt therefrom is that 'the first doctors who attempted to investigate the properties of opium . . . offered as an explanation . . . that it had a vis dormitiva or "soporific quality"'. (Wootton, *Social Science and Social Pathology*, p. 317.) This may well be so. Yet I wish that Wilson's pursuit of truth had gone so far as to ask whether the famous satirical references in Molière's comedy *Le Malade Imaginaire* constitute evidence sufficient to warrant Wilson's unqualified assertion that the 'mistake was actually committed by the first doctors who attempted to investigate the properties of opium'. (Wilson, pp. 43-4.)

3. A. G. N. Flew, 'Crime or Disease', in the *British Journal of Sociology* for March 1954. Some materials first processed there have been, with permission, recycled here.

4. J. R. Rees, *Mental Health and the Offender*, p. 6. This was no unrepeated aberration. For in the Foreword to the 3rd edition (1951) of *The Health of the Mind*, first published in 1929, he observes (p. 14) how now 'we are much more aware of the widespread incidence of emotional disturbances – the neuroses, psychosomatic illnesses, our increased delinquency rates – in addition to the psychoses, the figures for which remain more or less steady'.

5. Karl Menninger, *The Crime of Punishment*, p. 17. Some small punctuation changes have been made to ensure 'amicable coexistence': something which in this particular case – for once – is not achieved at the price of injustice to anyone.

6. Compare Francesco Carrara: 'Crime is not an entity in fact, but an entity in law.' (Quoted in Radzinowicz, *In Search of Criminology*, p. 180.)

According to the London *Times* this embarrassingly elementary point was missed, or at least muffed, at a recent conference of Directors of Criminological Research Institutes. For on 3 December 1971, under the headline 'Experts agree on a new definition of Crime', the *Times* correspondent reported from Strasbourg: 'Experts from 15 countries agreed that the only acceptable definition of crime was behaviour which seriously disturbed the life of society. . . . They noted that the concept of crime varied from country to country, and within the same society at different times.' They proceeded to remark, with approval, 'modern trends in dealing with shoplifting, worthless cheques, homosexuality, and abortion', which 'showed that such acts were no longer considered as true crimes. On the other hand, pollution of the environment, noise, and invasions of privacy were being treated more and more often as criminal offences.'

Even if, as one must hope, the fault here lay not among the massed criminologists but somewhere in the Thompson organisation, it will still be useful to explain again for present application the old familiar philosophers' distinction between connotation and denotation. The connotation of a word is the meaning of that word, whereas the denotation of the word is the objects to which it may correctly be applied. That the denotation of the word 'crime' varies thus with time and place constitutes no reason for saying that its connotation does, or should, vary correspondingly; and hence no reason for demanding or propounding new definitions for all the supposed new meanings supposedly generated by these variations. That the denotation of the word 'I' depends upon who is speaking or writing has no tendency to show that it is systematically ambiguous, or that a fresh definition is required every time that someone else learns English. That 'the morning star' and 'the evening star' happen to share the same denotation is not evidence that these two expressions are synonymous.

7. The *Syracuse Herald-Journal* for 27 March 1963, p. 35. Those who would prefer a more traditional example may reconsider St. Augustine's account of the disinterested wickedness of the theft of the pears: 'Nam decerpta projeci epulatus inde solam iniquitatem, quae laetabar fovens.' (*Confessions*, II 6.)

I owe the first of these references, and much else, to Dr Thomas Szasz [3], pp. 74–5. Although, as will appear later, I cannot agree with all his conclusions about *The Myth of Mental Illness*, I should like to say here how much I admire his crusading concern for the liberties, dignity and accountability of the human person.

8. D. H. Stott, *Delinquency and Human Nature*, pp. 351, 363 and 10; the third quotation was originally italicised.

9. All criminologists recognise, at least some of the time, that there must be 'many offences which never come to the notice of the police at all. This is the so-called "Dark Number" of crime. One can only guess at its size. That it is a substantial number is certain . . . it is possible that only one crime in twelve ultimately ends in a sentence by the courts.' (H. Jones, *Crime in a Changing Society*, pp. 15 and 18.) By the way: Stott is not the only criminologist inclined to derive conclusions about all without exception from evidence about some as opposed to others. For Howard Jones writes (ibid., p. 55); 'No longer, also, are mothers discouraged from visiting their sick children in hospital. . . . Following the recommendations to that effect of the Platt Committee, visits are now encouraged in many children's hospitals, though others find it difficult to break with the older, more austere tradition.'

10. I have examined some features of the position of Thrasymachus more closely in 'Must Morality Pay: what Socrates should have said to Thrasymachus', in *The Listener* for 1966; also in Flew [6], III 5.

11. Compare Plato, *Euthyphro* §§9E–11B; quoted and discussed in Flew [6], I 2.

12. *Report* [2], p. 2.

13. The 1957 Royal Commission fails to follow its own sensible term-inological recommendation to employ the expression 'disorders of the mind' to comprehend the two traditional contrasting categories of the 'mentally ill' and the 'mentally defective'. (Compare §§10 and 74, pp. 4 and 25.) This is of course a contrast which has, and is seen to have, a physical parallel. See Part II, Section 4, below.

Lasswell's paper is called 'What psychiatrists and political scientists can learn from each other'. The passage quoted is at p. 39; not p. 34, as stated by Szasz [3], p. 221.

14. Bertrand Russell, *The Practice and Theory of Bolshevism*, pp. 28–9. Any-one whose eyebrows rise at the suggestion that in his latest years Russell's sympathies were increasingly aligned with the Socialist Bloc and its causes will be equally surprised to read the last words of the message which he sent to Hanoi on 11 June 1966: 'I extend my warm regards and full solidarity for President Ho Chi Minh and for the people of Vietnam. I convey my great wish that the day may not be far off when a united and liberated Vietnam will celebrate its victory in a free Saigon.'

15. F. H. Bradley [2], p. 152 and ff.

16. For further explanation of the ideas of this paragraph see: either Flew [6], IV, especially 3; or Flew [2], 'Introduction'.

17. H. L. A. Hart, *Punishment and Responsibility*, p. 20.

18. T. S. Szasz [2], p. 70.

19. In the case of the recent edition of *Erewhon* for the Penguin English Library such hopes would be disappointed. Yet there can surely be very little point in furnishing a book of this kind with any introduction at all if the editor cannot seize the chance to discuss such central questions.

20. Szasz [3], p. 70.

21. Plato, *Republic*, §§325E–353E. Compare the conclusions about the three elements in the soul described in Section 8 of Part I of this essay (pp. 17–20).

22. Anyone wanting to go further with Plato in this direction can be referred to Anthony Kenny's 'Mental Health in Plato's *Republic*' in the *Proceedings of the British Academy* for 1969, pp. 229–53. Although I did not discover Kenny's paper until Part I was already complete, I must record that Kenny anticipated me by two years in the basic contention: 'The con-cept of mental health was Plato's invention.' (Ibid., p. 229.) It is perhaps also just worth noticing here that Plato, after first urging that curable in-justices should be cured 'as being diseases in the soul', then proceeded quite conventionally, as did Butler later, to suggest as the appropriate therapeutic measures the traditional penal sanctions (*Laws*, §862C-E).

23. M. Jahoda, *Current Concepts of Positive Mental Health*, pp. v, 3, and 109–110.

24. Ibid., p. 111.

25. Ibid., p. ix.

26. Ibid. See especially pp. 18–21 and 73–6.

27. K. Soddy (ed.), *Cross-Cultural Studies in Mental Health*, p. 59.

28. Ibid., p. 65.

29. Jahoda, p. 3.

30. Soddy, pp. 70 and 106. This tendency is noticed in their own way

by another International and Interprofessional Study Group convened by the World Federation for Mental Health: Soddy and Ahrenfeldt [2], pp. 152–4. Compare also Jahoda, pp. 78–9; Wootton, p. 220; and Soddy and Ahrenfeldt [1], pp. 95 ff.

31. Wootton, p. 203.

32. Ibid., p. 207.

33. Ibid., p. 240. Lady Wootton's argument was in fact accepted by the judges of England when they gave the answers to questions from the House of Lords from which the authority of the McNaghten Rules derives. The principle involed has certainly been followed in several Common Law jurisdictions. It has however traditionally been attacked by psychiatrists who deny that there are isolated delusions not symptomatic of some more general and fundamental disorder. In defence of the lawyers it should be pointed out that the judges in their answers were most careful to emphasise that they were following the contrary assumption; and it was this contrary assumption which was presented as the expert testimony at the original trial. See chapter VI of Sheldon Glueck [1]: the fourth question and answer, referring to Lady Wootton's point, are quoted in full on p. 169. Compare also Walker [2], chapter V. We are, I am glad to notice, agreed (p. 103) that 'if the judges' answers represented the law, McNaghten should have been convicted'. About this, as about so much else, Queen Victoria was right (ibid., pp. 188–92).

34. Wootton, p. 227.

35. Ibid., p. 289.

36. J. E. MacDonald, 'The Concept of Responsibility', in the *Journal of Mental Science* for 1955, pp. 715–16; quoted by Wootton, pp. 247–8. It is not often that the present writer is content to be brigaded with 'the religious and others of that kidney'! But it is, I am afraid, a case of one: 'Of whom to be dispraised were no small praise' (J. Milton, *Paradise Regained*, III 55).

37. Bernard Glueck, 'Changing Concepts in Forensic Psychiatry', in the *Journal of Criminal Law, Criminology and Police Science* for July – August 1954, pp. 127 and 130; quoted with comment by Wootton, p. 248.

38. See Note 13, above; which attaches to Section 9 of Part I.

39. This is a good moment to mention A. I. Melden's salutary monograph *Free Action*.

40. See Note 36, above, and the text to that note in Part II, Section 3 *ad fin.*

41. Lester King, in *Philosophy of Science* for 1954, Vol. XXI, p. 197. Compare too G. Caplan's statement in his *Principles of Preventive Psychiatry*: 'In our culture, the role of "patient" is associated with the idea of being the passive victim of some "illness"; even though a person is expected to help himself in the recovery process, it is felt that the main responsibility for his improvement rests with the doctors and nurses who "treat" him' (p. 102). It is one thing, and right, to say that the treatment of patients is culturally conditioned. It is another, and wrong, to suggest – as here – that whether a man who has a disease is or is not a victim of that disease depends on his culture.

42. Boethius, *The Consolations of Philosophy*, IV 6. The resemblance to Plato is not of course coincidental; for Boethius was steeped in Plato's dialogues as well as in the writings of Aristotle.

43. I owe thanks to my former colleague, Michael Akehurst of Keele, for drawing my attention to the article on 'Consent to Medical Treatment' by Diana M. Kloss in *Medicine, Science and the Law* for 1965, from which I learnt of the US case of *Hively* v. *Higgs* (1927) 253 p. 263. This decided that it was an offence to excise tonsils without the patient's consent and without positive evidence of severe pain. Appeal was made to the legal presumption that every bodily organ has some function beneficial to the organism. Presumably this presumption is defeasible in law as in biology. For it is apparently in fact defeated by the notorious falsifying instance of the vermiform appendix.

44. For an explanation both of the technical label and of the actual irrelevance to the problem of this common plea see Flew [4], §§2.30–2.31 and 2.42–2.58, especially 2.48.

45. J. L. Austin, *Philosophical Papers*, p. 140: this is in §3 of 'A Plea for Excuses', which first appeared in the *Proceedings of the Aristotelian Society* for 1956/7 and has been reprinted many times elsewhere.

46. Jahoda, p. 111.

47. Ibid., p. 111.

48. Karl Popper, *The Open Society and its Enemies*, chapter IX.

49. The possible gap between on the one hand what is allegedly in my interest or for my own good, and on the other hand what I myself actually want, can be of the greatest importance, both theoretically and practically. There is for instance much political wisdom to be derived from pondering a statement made by Abdul Kharume, First Vice-President of Tanzania. His government had recently rounded up all the unemployed of Dar-es-Salaam and posted them back home to their villages. At the birthday celebrations of the ruling – and of course the only legal – party on Saba Saba Day, he protested his uncomprehending innocence: 'Our government is democratic because it makes its decisions in the interests of and for the benefit of the people. I wonder why men who are unemployed are surprised and resentful at the Government . . . sending them back to the land for their own advantage.' See the Dar-es-Salaam press for the following morning 8 July 1967. One is reminded of the story of the three Boy Scouts who told their Scoutmaster that their good deed had been helping an old lady to cross the road. 'But why did it need three of you?' he asked. 'She didn't want to go.'

50. Which is exactly what does happen, left, right and centre. Consider for instance: 'A man . . . may be angrily against racial equality, public housing, the TVA [Tennessee Valley Authority] financial and technical aid to backward countries, organized labour, and the preaching of social rather than salvational religion. . . . Such people may appear 'normal' in the sense that they may be able to hold a job and otherwise maintain their status as members of society; but they are, we now recognize, well along the road toward mental illness.' (Overstreet, p. 115.) Compare, moving back from new left to old right, the no less pretentiously clinical and scientific claim: that 'Industrial unrest to a large degree means bad mental hygiene, and is to be corrected by good mental hygiene. The various antisocial attitudes that lead to crime are problems for the mental hygienist. Dependency, insofar as it is social parasitism not due to mental or physical defect,

belongs to mental hygiene.' (Quoted, from an unfortunately anonymous source, in Bromberg [1], p. 217.)

Two other examples are non-political. The first comes from Dr M. J. Rosenau's paper on 'Mental Hygiene and Public Health' in *Mental Hygiene* for 1935 (p. 9): 'The ultimate in mental hygiene means mental poise, calm judgement, and an understanding of leadership and fellowship – in other words, cooperation, with an attitude that tempers justice with mercy and humility.' The other is attributed to Dr O'Doherty: 'Mental health means a great deal more than mere absence of mental illness. . . . Among other things it demands good interpersonal relations with oneself [sic], with others, and with God.' (Quoted, presumably from one of the working papers prepared for his Scientific Committee, by Soddy, p. 73.)

51. Such discrediting by diagnosis is nowdays so popular as to demand a label: the argument, perhaps we should say, not *ad baculum* but *ad pulvinar* – not, that is, to the club but to the couch. For an amusing account of its archetypal employment within Freud's own Fellowship of the Ring, see Szasz [3], pp. 61–6.

52. Soddy, p. 70.

53. As a fairly complex exercise consider 'the dialectics of liberation' propounded by Herbert Marcuse. This is an egregiously horrid example. Its author scarcely tries to pretend that his special brand of revolutionary authoritarianism will be in the interests of those upon whom it is to be imposed, much less that they could themselves be induced to choose it. Thus in a notorious essay, fittingly given the Newspeak title 'Repressive Tolerance', Marcuse makes it about as plain as he ever makes anything that his revolution requires 'the dictatorship of an elite over the people'.

It is indeed a main grievance of Marcuse against the established capitalist order that the despised 'silent majority' does not want, and has no interest in, his revolution: 'By the same token, those minorities which strive for a change of the whole itself will . . . be left free to deliberate and discuss, to speak and to assemble . . . and will be left harmless and helpless in the face of the overwhelming majority, which militates against qualitative social change. This majority is firmly-grounded in the increasing satisfaction of needs, and technological and mental co-ordination, which testify to the general helplessness of radical groups in a well-functioning social system.' (Marcuse etc., pp. 134 and 107–8: the term 'Newspeak' comes from George Orwell's nightmare vision, *1984*.)

There would, as perhaps unwittingly Marcuse himself here implies, for sure be something very wrong with a set-up in which such Marcusian radicals had substantial power: it could not be, for that very reason, 'a well-functioning social system'.

54. Consider for example Sir Leslie Stephen's response to the charge that unbelief is essentially negative, whereas belief must be, commendably, positive: '. . . belief and unbelief are the very same thing. It is a mere question of convenience whether I shall express myself in negative or positive terms; whether I shall say "man is mortal" or "man is not immortal".' (L. Stephen, *An Agnostic's Apology*, p. 45.)

55. This was my own favourite message among those available on post-cards in campus stores in the U.S.A. during the academic year 1970/1. It

always, by contrast, reminded me of the title of one of the textbooks stacked in the bookshop on the University of Minnesota campus during the summer of 1954, *Psychology: the Science of Human Adjustment*. If there is to be an acceptable definition of 'mental health' in terms of adjustment, then 'adjustment' will have to be construed in the same sort of manner as it was earlier suggested that 'function' must be interpreted in the present context: not, that is, as a matter of behaving in this conformist as opposed to that nonconformist way; but rather as a matter of possessing some sort of capacity to cope – a capacity which may be actualised in various ways at the choice of the person in question. (See Part II, Section 4, above.) Unless this condition is met, mental health, conceived as adjustment, must become, what in fact it too often has been, yet another new verbal overcoat to cover the shabby, time-serving, principles of the Vicar of Bray. Compare Wootton, chapter VII, passim, but especially (iii).

56. These clauses, which are the ones always cited, come from the answer of the judges to questions two and three combined. The full text is given in Sheldon Glueck [1], pp. 178–9.

57. For this and other material on 'The History of the Legal Tests' compare Glueck [1], chapter V.

58. *Parsons v. State* (1886) 81 Ala. 5772 So 854.

59. J. F. Stephen [2], pp. 20–1. The brackets indicate the area of dispute. By the way: Weihofen (*Insanity as Defence in Criminal Law*, p. 411) confounds Sir James Fitzjames Stephen, the legal authority cited here, with Sir Leslie Stephen, cited in Note 54, above, Editor of the British *Dictionary of National Biography* and father of Virginia Woolf.

60. *Report* [1], p. 39: compare §317.

61. American Law Institute, 'Model Penal Code', §4.01 of the 1962 Official Draft.

62. *State v. Jones* (1871) 50 N.H. 369 and 394.

63. *Durham v. United States* (D.C. Cir. 1954) U.S. 214 F 2d 862.

64. De Reuck and Porter, *The Mentally Abnormal Offender*, p. 128.

65. And he is properly proud of the record of his institution in ensuring that that condition has not been satisfied (ibid., p. 128).

66. Abraham Goldstein of Yale Law School reminded the psychiatrist members of the same Symposium that the insanity defence 'has been notably unattractive to defendants (except when capital punishment was in prospect). . . . The reason, of course, is that the insanity defence usually brings not freedom but commitment for an entirely indeterminate period.' (Ibid., pp. 188–9.) Thus Daniel McNaghten himself – unlike the fictional anti-hero of Robert Traver's filmed novel *Anatomy of a Murder* – did not walk (or drive) from the court a free man after his acquittal as 'not guilty on the grounds of insanity'. Instead he spent the remaining twenty-two years of his life in continuous confinement. He eventually died in Broadmoor in 1865 of tuberculosis.

67. Here ponder the contribution of Dr N. Schipkowensky of the Psychiatric Clinic of the Medical Faculty of the University of Sofia: 'I am anxious about subjects who have not committed a crime but are potentially dangerous. In Bulgaria, Article 24 of the Penal Procedure Code provides for preventive treatment to protect both society and the subjects themselves

from the effects of their psychosis. Such treatment can be ordered only by the courts. . . . ' (De Reuck and Porter, p. 128.)

68. De Reuck and Porter, p. 183.

69. I recall especially some of the things written by Dr Henry Yellowlees out of his lifelong experience of the inhabitants of mental institutions (Yellowlees, *To Define True Madness*, chapter XIII and passim). Compare the classical statement of Pinel: 'I have nowhere met, expecting in romances, with fonder husbands, more affectionate parents, more impassioned lovers, more pure and exalted patriots, than in the lunatic asylum, during their intervals of calmness and reason.' (Pinel, p. 16.)

70. Freud [1], pp. 219–20: this is in Lecture XVII.

71. Ibid., p. 236: this is in Lecture XVIII.

72. For reasons already explained more fully in earlier sections of the present part II, Freud ought to have insisted that the symptoms of the mental illness are, not the outré performances as such, but the lack of control manifested therein. Consider here the theme of Arthur Koestler's novel *Arrival and Departure*, in which after a successful psychoanalysis the hero reverts to his previous revolutionary life-style; albeit no doubt with a greatly increased understanding and control of himself.

73. See my 'Motives and the Unconscious' in H. Feigl and M. Scriven (ed.), *The Foundations of Science and the Concepts of Psychology and Psychoanalysis* (Minneapolis: Minnesota UP, 1956). The quotation is at p. 155.

74. Szasz [1], p. 1.

75. Quoted, ibid., pp. 25–6: the original is at Freud [2], pp. 18–19.

76. Szasz [1], pp. 33–4; and compare the whole of chapter 1, passim.

77. Ibid., pp. 46–7.

78. Even in his most classical period Freud himself was capable of writing: ' . . . that we cannot dispense with the unconscious part of the mind in psychoanalysis, and that we are accustomed to deal with it as something actual and tangible.' (Freud [1], p. 235.) Compare T. R. Miles's *Eliminating the Unconscious*, an extremely helpful essay in reductive logical analysis.

79. Pinel, pp. 9 and 69.

80. This too I have argued at length in the paper mentioned in Note 73, above.

81. Consider how it is taken absolutely for granted in the statement: 'An asylum is no mysterious chamber of horrors, full of things dark and unspeakable. The slightest personal acquaintance with one dispels for ever all such absurd ideas; it is simply a hospital for the treatment of brain disease, and a home for those men and women whose diseases have baffled treatment.' (Yellowlees, p. 47.) Already in 1838 Dr Isaac Ray was insisting: 'Mania arises from a morbid affection of the brain. The progress of pathological anatomy during the present century has established this fact beyond the reach of a reasonable doubt.' (Ray, p. 104.)

82. Walker [1], p. 61.

83. Walker [2], p. 76.

84. The last clause is necessary since some psychiatrists seem to employ the term to mean something else, or perhaps nothing. Thus we read, of a man who had apparently spent his early manhood in the United States Navy: 'It is noteworthy that Wilton . . . had only become aware of his com-

pulsive homosexuality during the last ten years of his life (he was 42 when examined).' (Bromberg [2], p. 301.) The mind boggles, and the cheeks, blaze, at the thought of what might be made of this utterance by those who have served in the ships of the Queen.

For descriptions of some cases of kleptomania, straightforwardly construed, see Ray, pp. 140–3.

85. Wootton, p. 235. Sir William Blackstone was in his own way making a similar point when, apropos of the beginning of that practice of 'pious perjury' which we noticed in Section 2 of Part 1, he protested against juries behaving as if 'the very act of suicide is an evidence of insanity; as if every man who acts contrary to reason, had no reason at all'; and Blackstone added, with his usual hacking good sense, 'for the same argument would prove every other criminal non compos, as well as the self-murderer.' (Blackstone, IV p. 189.)

86. See, on the modern extension of the words 'clinic' and 'clinical' away from their original connection with the ideas of beds and being bedridden, Wootton, pp. 242 ff.

87. The material for this and the previous paragraph is borrowed from the valuable Appendix to Dr Karl Menninger (etc.) *The Vital Balance*.

88. 'Of course one thing he could do would be to live continently: there are millions of heterosexually inclined people who are continent for one reason or another, and this should be no more difficult for a homosexually inclined individual.' (Ibid., p. 196.) This unfashionable insistence upon the possibility of self-control is even more relevant in other contexts, in which there is not at present any equivalent of the Pill available to reduce the price of 'our pleasant vices'. It has also been noted for use in evidence against its author in Part III.

89. Freud [3], p. 3.

90. For instance: 'The perversions are . . . anatomical transgressions of the bodily regions destined for sexual union. . . .' (Ibid., p. 15.)

91. Wilbur and Muensterberger, *Psychoanalysis and Culture*, pp. 252–3. I could, but will not, forbear to quote Sir Winston Churchill: ' . . . restrict as much as possible the work of these gentlemen, who are capable of doing an immense amount of harm with what may very easily degenerate into charlatanry. The tightest hand should be kept over them, and they should not be allowed to quarter themselves in large numbers upon the Fighting Services at the public's expense.' (Churchill, *The Second World War*, IV p. 815.)

92. See Note 59, above, and text to that note in Section 7.

93. To be strictly fair, and perhaps almost more damaging, it has to be said that Dr Eissler does actually cite one single and singular case of detected malingering—as he maintains—'rapidly changing into a malignant psychosis.' He then proceeds directly to his unreservedly universal conclusion, already quoted, that 'malingering is always the sign of a disease'. (Wilbur and Muensterberger. p. 252.)

94. Menninger (etc.), p. 208: the italics are all, and all of, his. The first person to make this sort of suggestion seems to have been the German psychiatrist Ganser. For a description of his 'Ganser Syndrome' see Noyes, pp. 505–6.

95. This is provided by Dr Harry F. Darling in his article 'Definition of 'Psychopathic Personality' in the *Journal of Nervous and Mental Disease* for February 1945, at p. 125. I owe this reference to Lady Wootton.

96. Report [2] 'Minutes of Evidence', Eighth Day, p. 287.

97. Ibid., Thirtieth Day, p. 1225. The witness was Dr W. A. Heaton-Ward, Medical Superintendent of Stoke Park Hospital.

98. Margolis, *Psychotherapy and Morality*, p. 111. I quote here merely to provide an occasion to mention this book, and especially to recommend its immediately subsequent criticism of Edmund Bergler's egregious essay *Homosexuality: Disease or Way of Life*. Bergler shows the paternalistic effrontery of the psychiatrist as Guardian by maintaining (p. 9): 'Homosexuality is not the way of life these sick people gratuitously assume it to be, but a neurotic distortion of the total personality.'

99. De Reuck and Porter, p. 122.

100. Wootton, p. 250.

101. Ibid., p. 251.

102. Ibid., p. 253.

103. Ibid., p. 238. The quotation comes from a paper by Dr Aubrey Lewis on 'Health as a Social Concept' in the *British Journal of Sociology* for 1953. Dr Lewis stands out among his psychiatric colleagues for his clear appreciation of some of the pitfalls which beset this notion of mental disease.

104. J. Glover, *Responsibility*, pp. 137 and 138: hearts, by the way, must warm to an author who lets pass the misprint 'pre-martial sex' (p. 189). Compare Stafford-Clark, pp. 117-20.

105. Walker [1], p. 87.

106. It seems that the effluxion of the first twenty years after the first of these two statements was made brought no improvement in the situation: see, again, Walker [1], p. 87.

107. Menninger, p. 254: his italics, here and later.

108. Ibid., p. 256. Bradley's dictum will be quoted, once again, below.

109. Menninger, p. 257.

110. The qualification is necessary since both National Socialist and Leninist Socialist regimes from the beginning explicitly repudiated ideals embodied in the Hippocratic Oath. For the latter which, unlike the former, still persist and proliferate see for instance Field, *Doctor and Patient in Soviet Russia*, pp. 173 ff., and passim.

111. On the degeneration, in what one of my most cross-grained graduate students used to call 'this Age of the Busybody', of the word 'client' see Lady Wootton's wickedly entertaining chapter IX, 'Contemporary Attitudes in Social Work'. One cannot, she muses (p. 289), 'easily imagine any social worker's "client" saying "I must get hold of the services of a caseworker" as he might say: "I must find a doctor or a solicitor".'

112. Eysenck, who is so rightly sharp about the lack of hard evidence to support the therapeutic claims of the psychoanalysts, fails to take this point. In his *Crime and Personality*, he seems to notice no difference: between on the one hand the employment of conditioning to cure a patient who wants to be cured of enuresis (pp. 166–7); and on the other hand the inescapable 'brain-washing' of hostile prisoners of war (p. 181).

113. The standard example of such continuity and even intensification

through revolutionary change is that chronicled by Alexis de Tocqueville's classic *L'Ancien Régime*. A fictitious and frivolous case is perhaps more appropriate to our immediate concerns. Two male homosexuals were admiring the passage of the current Playmate of the Month: 'She almost makes one wish one were a Lesbian.'

114. Coke, *Third Institute*, chapter I.

115. Bradley [1], pp. 26–7. Things look a little different to those scientists to whom the very word 'justice' is an irritant: 'That he or she has broken the law gives us a technical reason for acting on behalf of society to try to do something that will lead him to react more acceptably, and which will protect the environment in the meantime.' (Menninger, p. 18.) For some recent philosophical discussion, see Acton, *The Philosophy of Punishment*, passim. Another and especially relevant piece, which I hope will soon be similarly anthologised somewhere, is Alf Ross, 'The Campaign against Punishment'. This is at present buried in *Scandinavian Studies in Law* for 1970, pp. 111–48. By the way: anyone proposing to write a well-nourished book on *The Roots of Crime* really ought to learn what the lex talionis is. For 'castration . . . for some sexual offences' is a case; not of an eye for an eye, a tooth for a tooth, but of 'if your (or, rather, his) eye (penis) offends thee (her, they should) pluck it out (off)''. See E. Glover, *The Roots of Crime* p. 389.

116. For the classical development of such thoughts, see Thomas Hobbes, *Leviathan*, especially chapter XIII; and compare Flew [3], pp. 163 ff. Since the nomological notion of cause is essentially connected with such subjunctive conditionals it was, quite simply, absurd for Mr A. J. P. Taylor to pontificate that members of his profession must never be concerned with what might have been: 'The historian should never dogmatize about what did not happen. We are not entitled to say that war would have been over sooner if Brooke's advice had been followed more closely. . . . Maybe so: maybe not. The experiment was not tried; therefore we can never tell.' (Review of Lord Alanbrooke's diaries, in the *Manchester Guardian* for 2 November 1959.) On the general point about the notion of cause see Flew [1], chapter VI.

117. See Note 66, above; and compare again Hart, chapters I and VII.

118. (1966). 49 Misc. 2d 533, 267 N.Y.S. 2d 920 (Ct Cl.)

119. Soddy, p. 186.

120. Plato, *The Republic*, §414; and compare Sections 8 and 10 of Part I, above.

121. See 'The Frontal Lobes' by Gösta Rylander in, I think, the *Annals of the Royal Norwegian Medical Association*, Vol. XXVII, p. 696. (I have not been able to check this reference, which I take from notes made when I first read this article in the early 1950s).

122. Ogden, *The ABC of Psychology*, p. 43. The learned Ogden here supplied no reference. Search both in Fulton's massive biography of Cushing, and then in the more hopeful papers listed there, was abortive.

123. Skinner, *Beyond Freedom and Dignity*, p. 19, and passim.

124. Originally in the *Twentieth Century* for 1954, and later in Lewis, *Undeceptions*, pp. 242–3.

125. Yet this point was completely mistaken by Ernest Jones; following Freud [3], XII, §2. See my paper in C. Hanly and M. Lazerowitz (eds.), *Psychoanalysis and Philosophy* (New York: International UP, 1970). Compare

G. B. Thomas, 'He Could Not Have Chosen Otherwise' in the *Southern Journal of Philosophy* for Winter 1967. The point was made earlier by J. F. Stephen [1], II pp. 102–3: according to Bradley [1], p. 48, by Hegel; and, in effect, by Aristotle in the *Nicomachean Ethics* III (i).

126. This basic liberal principle is too often overridden by psychiatrists in their more missionary moments. Consider for example the assertion, taken as too obvious for argument: 'If we establish that prostitution is a sign of backwardness, it is incumbent on the State to use every device, psychological and sociological, to remedy the defect.' (E. Glover, p. 262.)

127. Menninger, p. 136. As the punctation indicates, these words are here put into the mouth of a dialogue character. But there is no reason to think that Dr Menninger would repudiate them. The same unsound principle provides the nerve of one of the crucial arguments in *Homosexuality: Disease or Way of Life* (Bergler, pp. 7–9). It was also basic in the final psychiatric report in the case of James Cooper, pp. 90–1, below.

128. Quoted in Szasz [2], p. 249.

129. Glueck [1], p. 64. The author's outraged comment on the following page is too good – or too bad – to miss: 'This woman . . . was released on probation! Since then, she has worked in a factory for six months, on a job provided by the probation officer, but has again been arrested, for the same offence, and probation has again been recommended.' Contrast that with this recent and more open-eyed assessment: 'For the young woman of health and vitality, with little inclination for employment entailing hard work, long hours and a comparatively small salary, the attractions of prostitution are great. Such a woman is unlikely to listen to pleas as to the uncertainty of the future, for no employment which she would find agreeable, or in which she would be likely to be retained for any length of time, would offer greater security, financially or emotionally.' (Smith, *Women in Prison*, p. 40.)

130. Berg [2], p. 190.

131. Not all of us however would approve forcible commitment to a mental hospital as the final preventive. Contrast Dr F. J. Braceland, quoted in Szasz [2], p. 61. Braceland claims nevertheless to be 'just as much interested in people's rights as anyone else'.

132. See Dr F. Wiseman on 'Psychiatry and Law: Use and Abuse of Psychiatry in a Murder Case' in the *American Journal of Psychiatry* for October 1961; and compare Szasz [2], pp. 154–8.

133. Yet another argument which should be accorded more weight than it usually is, is that any extension of the scope of the criminal law to cover gambling, private sexual deviations and other 'crimes without victims' must involve some diversion of enforcement effort which would be better directed to the basic task of protecting the public from violence and robbery. See for instance Hawkins and Morris, *The Honest Politician's Guide to Crime Control*, chapter 1. By the way: while I appreciate their use of material from my 'Theology and Falsification' in a typically forceful and entertaining attack on the myth of an invisible empire of crime, I still believe that such quotations ought to be acknowledged. (Ibid, pp. 211–12; compare Flew and MacIntyre *New Essays in Philosophical Theology*, pp. 96–9.)

134. Szasz [2], pp. 84–5 and 200–4.

135. The most comprehensive secondary source known to me, and that

in which authority for all my statements can be found, is the first part of a two-part review article by I. F. Stone: 'Betrayal by Psychiatry' in the *New, York Review of Books*, Vol. xviii, No. 2 (10 December 1972).

136. This suggests an interpretation of an enigmatic and disturbing statement in one of the classics: ' . . . persons practically acquainted with the insane mind' are well aware 'that in every hospital for the insane are patients capable of distinguishing between right and wrong, knowing well enough how to appreciate the nature and legal consequences of their acts, acknowledging the sanctions of religion, and never acting from irresistible impulses, but deliberately and shrewdly.' The author asks: 'Is all this to be utterly ignored in courts of justice?' (Ray, . . . *Medical Jurisprudence of Insanity*, p. 344.) Could it be that he was feeling his way towards some new category of the alien as a possible condition to defeat imputations of criminal responsibility?

137. H. Jones, *Crime in a Changing Society*, p. 51.

138. As was in fact done by Dr Snezhnevsky in response to an intervention by the physicists Peter Kapitza and Andrei Sakharov. The same Dr Snezhnevsky as leader of the Soviet delegation to the Mexico City conference of the World Psychiatric Association was later charged with the task of ensuring that the conference should not respond to appeals for help from Sakharov and others; an assignment which, thanks particularly to the co-operation of the top brass of American psychiatry, he was able to fulfil.

139. Compare the September–October 1964 issue of *Fact* magazine on 'The Unconscious of a Conservative'. This reported the response of nearly 20 per cent of the 12,000 plus psychiatrists of the U.S.A. to such questions as: 'Do you believe Barry Goldwater is psychologically fit to serve as President of the United States?' They cast their postal diagnoses two to one against Goldwater. This willingness of so many to present their political as their professional judgement ought to disturb even those who might agree with the former. Perhaps too it throws light on the unresponsiveness indicated in the previous note: those who live in glass-houses do well to frown on the throwing of stones.

140. E. Jones [2], iii p. 98.

141. Menninger, pp. 96–7: punctuation assimilated.

142. De Reuck and Porter, p. 183.

143. Stott, p. 7: 'Albert! not in front of the servants!'

144. See Note 88, above.

145. Boswell's *Journal* for 10 October 1769.

146. Lange, *Crime as Destiny*, p. 14.

147. Freud [3], pp. 162 and 148; compare Freud [2], iv p. 388.

148. Brill, *Psychoanalytic Psychiatry*, p. 87.

149. E. Jones [1], ii, pp. 181–2: the passage climaxes in the misunderstanding of Luther mentioned in Note 125, above.

150. A point nicely made by St Augustine in the *De Libero Arbitrio*, iii (iii). The contrary error is, according to Bradley, an element in 'The Vulgar Notion of Responsibility'. Bradley writes of his plain man: 'If I am right, he would be inclined to say, "The growth of my character has been predicted when I was not; and how then can I have had anything to do with it?" . . . If, from given data and from universal rules, another man can work out the

generation of him, like a sum in arithmetic, where is his self gone to . . . To explain the origin of a man is utterly to annihilate him.' (Bradley [1], pp. 17 and 20.)

151. On the unsoundness of such apparently seductive arguments, see Flew [6], vii 5. The crucial distinction between what is said in the two clauses in the text is made and denied in successive lines of *Measure for Measure* (Act ii, Sc. 2):

> Angelo: I will not do it
> Isabella: But can you if you would?
> Angelo: Look, what I will not, that I cannot do.

152. Something very like this final paragraph of Section 2 originally appeared in my 'Splitting Hairs before Starting Hares' in *The Personalist* for Winter 1972. Other materials from the same source have also, with permission, been recycled into the present essay. For more on first such psychic determinism and then its implications, see the papers mentioned in Notes 73 and 125, above.

153. Eysenck, p. 183.

154. How else could we respond for instance to the breathtaking revelations of B. F. Skinner, doyen of American behavioural psychologists? Under the suitably agressive title *Beyond Freedom amd Dignity* he crusades against outworn superstition. A truly scientific behavioural technology will have no room, it seems, for any anthropomorphic ideas about man: 'Although physics soon stopped personifying things . . . it continued for a long time as if they had wills, impulses, feelings, purposes, and other fragmentary attributes of an unwilling agent. . . . All this was eventually abandoned, and to good effect. . . .' Yet, deplorably, 'the behavioral sciences still appeal to comparable internal states'. We cannot therefore be surprised, although we are supposed to regret, that 'Almost everyone who is concerned with human affairs– as political scientist, philosopher, man of letters, economist, psychologist, linguist, sociologist, theologian, anthropologist, educator, or psychotherapist – continues to talk about human behaviour in this prescientific way.' (Skinner, pp. 8 and 9.) Noam Chomsky does a splendid hatchet job in the *New York Review of Books*, Vol. xvii, No. 11 (30 December 1971.)

155. Descartes, *Principles of Philosophy*, 1 (xl) and (xli). One modern discussion of this inference is between C. A. Campbell, C. K. Grant and J.J.C. Smart in *Mind* for 1951, 1952 and 1961. The special case in which a man 'shows his freedom' by falsifying some prediction about his own conduct was neatly treated in a long note in Hume's first *Inquiry*, viii (i); and much earlier during the Italian Renaissance, as the well-read Hume perhaps knew, by Lorenzo Valla in his dialogue 'On Freewill'. It may therefore provoke interesting reflections to notice that one of our Oxford contemporaries recently credited the discovery of this case to another, the present Warden of Wadham. (J. Glover, p. 26.)

56. Luther, *De Servo Arbitrio*, v (viii).

157. Ibid., v (vi). The passage continues: 'It is not for us to inquire into these Mysteries, but to adore them. If flesh and blood take offence here and grumble, well, let them grumble; they will achieve nothing; grumbling will

not change God! And however many of the ungodly stumble and depart, the elect will remain (cf. *John*, VI 60 ff.)'

158. Ibid., II (viii). That Aquinas recognised substantially the same implications of the same theist premises can be seen in the *Summa contra Gentiles*, III 67, 88–9, and 152–3; and compare Flew [4], §§2.34–2.41.

159. *De Servo Arbitrio*, II (vii).

160. Lucas, *The Freedom of the Will*, p. 12; and compare p. 27.

161. It would, generally, be an enormous step forward if everyone thinking of bursting into print in this area would first settle down to a short but catholic course of classical reading. One excellent programme would be to study the relevant sections of all the works mentioned in Schopenhauer's prize essay on 'The Freedom of the Will'; and then to follow this with one or two contemporary collections, such as Hook. Equipped by this modest propaideutic, the author of a book on *Fate, Logic and Time* would not, while fresh out of an Ivy League graduate school, take it absolutely for granted that: if a 'man has freewill', in the sense of the 'power to perform . . . actions other than those which he does, in fact, perform'; then, 'consequently, certain human actions are inherently unpredictable .' (Cahn, pp. 1 and 3.) Nor again would an acute and well-established Oxford philosopher, speaking of the idea that Determinism and action are compatible, broadcast the observation that this is a thesis 'which in fact has had sponsors here and there since at least the time of Hobbes.' (G. J. Warnock, in Pears (ed.), *Freedom and the Will*, p. 70.) For this is not quite how one describes what one knows to have been maintained not only by Hobbes but also in their various ways by Locke and by Leibniz, by Hume and by Mill; to say nothing of Aquinas, of Luther and of Jonathan Edwards.

162. Again, in the *De Servo Arbitrio*, Luther chides 'the mistake, that, in the matter of merits and rewards, we ponder unprofitable thoughts and questions about worthiness (which is non-existent) when we ought to be discussing consequence alone. Hell and the judgement of God await the wicked as a necessary consequence' (II (xv).) Compare, both here and immediately below, 'Freedom and Resentment' in Strawson (ed.), *Studies in the Philosophy of Thought and Action*.

163. Bromberg and Halleck, *Psychiatric Aspects of Criminology*, pp. 66–7. The author cited, M. D. Wolfgang, is a sociologist rather than a psychiatrist, urging that the members of his own particular academic craft union should also have a cut of the action. So he concludes: 'if determinism is the appropriate approach . . . then morethan a psychic determinism is required'; for every man 'is the product of the social system that helps him to develop his capacities legitimately or that forces him to use them illegitimately. . . .' (Ibid., pp. 69–70.) This is a very typical cheat: a universal Determinism cannot thus discriminate in favour of the criminal.

164. Mottram, *The Physical Basis of Personality*, p. 115. From whom?

165. Lucas, pp. 110 and 114. I have developed the contrary argument in 'A Rational Animal' in J. R. Smythies (ed.), *Brain and Mind* (London: Routledge and Kegan Paul, 1965).

166. Sheldon Glueck [2], p. 6.

167. Lucas, pp. 20 and 27.

168. Hume, *A Treatise of Human Nature*, Introduction.

169. C. Lombroso, *Crime: Its Causes and Remedies*, p. 380. I have been unable to trace a copy of Rondeau's work in either the British Museum or the catalogue of the Bibliothèque Nationale. Lombroso is himself requoting from a fellow Italian, It would be mean not to share with those who may never have occasion to read Lombroso the thought (p. 196): 'In France the greatest tendency to sexual crimes is found among the shoemakers, – a fact to be referred to their alcoholism, and to the effect upon their genital organs of their position while at work.'

170. C. Darrow, *Crime: Its Cause and Treatment*, pp. *v*, 96, and 117.

171. Quoted by Walker [2], p. 89.

172. Bradley [2], pp. 155 and 156: 'Some Remarks on Punishment' was first published in 1894.

173. See for example Neustatter, *Psychological Disorder and Crime*.

174. K. Friedlander, *The Psychoanalytic Approach to Juvenile Delinquency*, p. 193. I should perhaps say, although I do not think it affects any issues at this point, that she is supposed to be meaning by 'delinquent' anyone whose 'attitude towards society is such that it will eventually lead to a violation of the law'. (p. 77)

175. Berg [1], p. 36: punctuation assimilated.

176. M. Balint 'On Punishing Offenders', in Wilbur and Muensterberger, p. 262.

177. Dr Edward Glover talks (p. 76) of 'the seeming [sic] paradox that the criminal who inflicts suffering on society is himself a victim of unconscious suffering'. Can unfelt pains offset real sufferings?

178. Bradley [1], p. 48: italics removed.

179. Bromberg [2], p. 50: the sneer quotes are his.

180. Dostoievsky, *Crime and Punishment*, 1 2.

Bibliography

Note. This is not intended to include any work not mentioned somewhere in either the text or the notes. It also omits literary and other classics available in several differently paginated editions, since in these cases it seemed better to use whatever edition-neutral method of reference is available.

ACTON, H. B. (ed.), *The Philosophy of Punishment* (London: Macmillan 1967).

AUSTIN, J. L., *Philosophical Papers* (Oxford: Clarendon 1961).

BERG, C., [1] *War in the Mind* (London: Macaulay 1941).

——— [2] *Deep Analysis* (London: Allen and Unwin 1946).

BERGLER, E., *Homosexuality: Disease or Way of Life* (New York: Hill and Wang 1956).

BLACKSTONE, Sir William, *Commentaries on the Laws of England* (Oxford: OUP 1769).

BRADLEY, F. H., [1] *Ethical Studies* (Oxford: OUP, 2nd edn 1927).

——— [2] *Collected Papers* (Oxford: Clarendon 1935).

BRILL, A. A., *Psychoanalytic Psychiatry* (New York: Lehmann 1948).

BROMBERG, W., [1] *The Mind of Man* (London: Hamilton 1937).

——— [2] *Crime and the Mind* (New York and London: Macmillan and Collier-Macmillan 1965).

BROMBERG, W., and HALLECK, S. L., *Psychiatric Aspects of Criminology* (Springfield, Illinois: C. C. Thomas 1968).

CAHN, S. M., *Fate, Logic and Time* (New Haven: Yale UP 1967).

CAPLAN, G., *Principles of Preventive Psychiatry* (London: Tavistock Press 1964).

CHURCHILL, W. S., *The Second World War* (London: Cassell 1948–54).

COKE, E., *The Third Part of the Institutes of the Laws of England* (London: Lee and Pakeman 1644).

DARROW, C., *Crime: its Cause and Treatment* (London: C. A. Watts 1934).

DE REUCK, A. V. S., and PORTER, R., *The Mentally Abnormal Offender* (Boston: Little, Brown 1968).

EYSENCK, H. J., *Crime and Personality* (London: Paladin 1970).

FIELD, M. G., *Doctor and Patient in Soviet Russia* (Cambridge, Mass.: Harvard UP 1957

FLEW, A. G. N., [1] *Hume's Philosophy of Belief* (London and New York: Routledge and Kegan Paul, and Humanities Press 1961).

——— [2] *Body, Mind and Death* (New York and London: Macmillan and Collier-Macmillan 1964).

——— [3] 'Thomas Hobbes' in D. J. O'Connor (ed.) *A Critical History of Western Philosophy* (New York and London: Free Press of Glencoe, and Allen and Unwin 1964).

FLEW, A. G. N., [4] *God and Philosophy* (London and New York: Hutchinson and Harcourt Brace 1966. Also New York: Dell Delta Paperbacks 1967).

—— [5] *Evolutionary Ethics* (London: Macmillan 1967).

—— [6] *An Introduction to Western Philosophy* (London and Indianapolis: Thames and Hudson, and Bobbs-Merrill 1971).

FLEW, A. G. N., and MACINTYRE, A. (eds.), *New Essays in Philosophical Theology* (London and New York: SCM Press and Macmillan 1955).

FREUD, S., [1] *Introductory Lectures on Psychoanalysis* (London: Allen and Unwin 1922).

—— [2] *Collected Papers* (London: Hogarth 1948–50).

—— [3] *The Psychopathology of Everyday Life* (Harmondsworth: Penguin 1938).

—— [4] *Three Contributions to the Theory of Sex* (New York: Dutton 1962).

FRIEDLANDER, K., *The Psychoanalytic Approach to Juvenile Delinquency* (London and New York: Routledge and Kegan Paul, and International UP 1947 and 1960).

FULTON, J. F., *Harvey Cushing* (Springfield: Thomas 1946).

GLOVER, E., *The Roots of Crime* (New York: International UP 1960).

GLOVER, J. *Responsibility* (London and New York: Routledge and Kegan Paul, and Humanities Press 1970).

GLUECK, S., [1] *Mental Disorder and the Criminal Law* (Boston: Little, Brown 1925).

—— [2] *Law and Psychiatry* (Baltimore and London: Johns Hopkins UP, and Fairstock 1962 and 1963).

HART, H. L. A., *Punishment and Responsibility* (Oxford: Clarendon 1968).

HAWKINS, G., and Morris, N., *The Honest Politician's Guide to Crime Control* (Chicago: Chicago UP 1970).

HOOK, S. (ed.), *Determinism and Freedom in the Age of Modern Science* (New York: New York UP 1958).

JACOBS, F. G. *Criminal Responsibility* (London: Weidenfeld and Nicolson 1971).

JAHODA, M., *Current Concepts of Positive Mental Health* (New York: Basic Books 1958).

JONES, E., [1] *Essays in Applied Psychoanalysis* (London: Hogarth 1951).

—— [2] *Sigmund Freud* (London: Hogarth 1954–7).

JONES, H., *Crime in a Changing Society* (Harmondsworth: Penguin 1965).

LANGE, J., *Crime as Destiny* (London: Allen and Unwin 1931).

LEWIS, C. S., *Undeceptions* (London: Geoffrey Bles 1972).

LOMBROSO, C., *Crime: its Causes and Remedies* (Montclair, NJ: Patterson-Smith 1968. Italian original 1906).

LUCAS, J. R., *The Freedom of the Will* (Oxford: Clarendon 1970).

MARCUSE, H., MOORE, B., and WOLFF, R. P., *A Critique of Pure Tolerance* (London: Cape 1969).

MARGOLIS, J., *Psychotherapy and Morality* (New York: Random House, 1966).

MAUDSLEY, H., *Responsibility in Mental Disease* (London: Kegan Paul 1872).

MELDEN, A. I., *Free Action* (London: Routledge and Kegan Paul 1961).

MENNINGER, K., *The Crime of Punishment* (New York: Viking Press 1968).

MENNINGER, K., with MAYMAN, M., and PRUYSER, P., *The Vital Balance* (New York: Viking Press 1963).

MICHAEL, J., and WECHSLER, H., *Criminal Law and its Administration* (Brooklyn, NY: Foundation Press 1941).

MILES, T. R., *Eliminating the Unconscious* (London: Pergamon Press 1966).

MOTTRAM, V. H., *The Physical Basis of Personality* (Harmondsworth: Penguin 1944).

NEUSTATTER, W. L., *Psychological Disorder and Crime* (London: Christopher Johnson 1953).

NOYES, A. P., *Modern Clinical Psychiatry* (Philadelphia: Saunders, 4th edn 1956).

OGDEN, C. K., *The ABC of Psychology* (Harmondsworth: Penguin 1944).

OVERSTREET, H. A., *The Great Enterprise* (New York: Norton 1952).

PEARS, D. F. (ed.), *Freedom and the Will* (London: Macmillan 1963).

PINEL, P., *A Treatise on Insanity* (New York: Hafner 1962 – facsimile of the first English edition of 1806).

POPPER, Sir Karl, *The Open Society and its Enemies* (London: Routledge 1945).

RADZINOWICZ, L., *In Search of Criminology* (London: Heinemann 1961).

RAY, I., *A Treatise on the Medical Jurisprudence of Insanity* (Cambridge, Mass.: Belknap 1962. First edition 1838).

REES, J. R., [1] *Mental Health and the Offender* (London: Clarke Hall Fellowship 1947).

———— [2] *The Health of the Mind* (London: Faber, 3rd edn 1951).

RUSSELL, B. A. W., *The Practice and Theory of Bolshevism* (London: Allen and Unwin, 2nd edn 1949).

SKINNER, B. F., *Beyond Freedom and Dignity* (New York: Knopf 1971).

SMITH, A. D., *Women in Prison* (London: Stevens 1962).

SODDY, K. (ed.), *Cross-Cultural Studies in Mental Health* (London: Tavistock Press 1961).

SODDY, K., and AHRENFELDT, R. H., [1] *Mental Health in a Changing World* (London: Tavistock Press 1965).

———— [2] *Mental Health and Contemporary Thought* (London: Tavistock Press 1967).

———— [3] *Mental Health in the Service of the Community* (London: Tavistock Press 1967).

STAFFORD-CLARK, D., *Psychiatry Today* (Harmondsworth: Penguin, 2nd edn 1963).

STEPHEN, Sir James Fitzjames, [1] *A History of the Criminal Law of England* (London: Macmillan 1883).

———— [2] *A Digest of the Criminal Law* (London: Macmillan, 6th edn 1904).

STEPHEN, Sir Leslie, *An Agnostic's Apology* (London: Smith Elder 1893).

STOTT, D. H., *Delinquency and Human Nature* (Dunfermline: Carnegie United Kingdom Trust 1950).

STRAWSON, P. F. (ed.), *Studies in the Philosophy of Thought and Action* (London: Oxford UP 1968).

SZASZ, T. S., [1] *The Myth of Mental Illness* (New York: Harper and Row 1961).

———— [2] *Law, Liberty and Psychiatry* (New York: Macmillan 1963).

———— [3] *Ideology and Insanity* (New York: Doubleday Anchor 1970).

WALKER, N., [1] *Crime and Punishment in Britain* (Edinburgh: Edinburgh UP 1965).
———— [2] *Crime and Insanity in England* (Edinburgh: Edinburgh UP 1968).
WEIHOFEN, H., *Insanity as a Defence in Criminal Law* (New York and London: Commonwealth Fund and Oxford UP 1933).
WILBUR, G. B., and MUENSTERBERGER, W., *Psychoanalysis and Culture* (New York: International UP 1951).
WILSON, J., *Language and the Pursuit of Truth* (Cambridge: CUP 1956).
WOOTTON, B., *Social Science and Social Pathology* (London: Allen and Unwin 1959).
YELLOWLEES, H., *To Define True Madness* (London: Sidgwick and Jackson 1953).
Report: [1] *The Royal Commission on Capital Punishment* (London: HMSO 1953).
———— [2] *The Royal Commission on the Law Relating to Mental Illness and Mental Deficiency* (London: HMSO 1957).

Index of Personal Names

This covers only pp. xxiii-132 inclusive; and it does not include the names of Gods or of fictitious human persons.

LaVergne, TN USA
05 February 2010
172229LV00004B/25/P